MW01242663

Finding Grace

Crystal L. Hultquist

authorHOUSE®

AuthorHouse™
1663 Liberty Drive
Bloomington, IN 47403
www.authorhouse.com
Phone: 1-800-839-8640

First published by AuthorHouse 1/25/2010

ISBN: 978-1-4490-6520-1 (e)
ISBN: 978-1-4490-6519-5 (sc)
ISBN: 978-1-4490-6521-8 (hc)

Library of Congress Control Number: 2009913738

Printed in the United States of America
Bloomington, Indiana

This book is printed on acid-free paper.

Dedication

This book is dedicated to my mother, who I never really gave the chance to know me. May one day, she understand how I became who I am.

Acknowledgements

This book would not have a beginning or end if it wasn't for my friend and mentor in this process, Florence Weinberg. Thank you for your knowledge, your time and your encouragement. To my sweet friend and colleague, Maggie Hanson, who joined me on this journey of writing and listened with much love as my story unfolded, thank you 'mom'. To Gerry Grace, may great things happen with this story and may our friendship grow because of it. Finally, to my husband, 'Dr. Sir', you were so open to this project and supported me every step of the way. I could not ask for anything more. You are everything I need.

Foreword
Gerard Grace, Ph. D., M. Div.

It started out like any other typical hospice day: gather together with the interdisciplinary team at 8 AM and listen to the night report. The night report usually directed the operations of the day; some patients may have died, some may have been in uncontrollable pain, other family members may have been in severe grief or emotional and psychic pain at the imminent loss of their loved one, and for other families the anxiety of the dying process may have opened up vulnerable areas connected with old wounds in their family history that needed tending to.

This particular day there was a call in for a chaplain to visit a dying patient and perform a ritual of baptism. There happened to be a new employee starting that day—Crystal, a nurse with much hospice experience behind her. Crystal was being oriented to the culture of this new hospice company. I was to be the chaplain who would respond to the baptism call, and it was suggested that Crystal, the new nurse, accompany me as part of her orientation and also to address any clinical issues pertaining to the patients' pain, medications, or educational needs. By midday the stitch that kept Crystal's life's tapestry in place would unravel at the seams, and our working relationship would take on a whole new meaning and significance. This book is a heart-rending and inspirational account of that unraveling and the subsequent reweaving of a new tapestry buttressed by hope, new meaning, spiritual revival, and emotional resilience.

People who have been victims of traumatic experiences usually organize their lives in such a way that they avoid situations, people, or places that might remind them of the original trauma or painful event. This avoidance strategy is a necessary coping mechanism that protects the person from intolerable levels of anxiety associated with thoughts, images, and feelings connected with the original trauma. Certain contexts, situations, people, sounds, and other tactical stimuli will act as triggers to the original trauma, thereby activating the anxiety response marked by the fight, flight, or freeze syndrome. Avoidance is the natural mechanism to decrease this exposure and avoid the pain.

Avoidance, while effective in the short term, will never be a long-term solution. The longer the avoidance is maintained, the deeper the negative feelings are buried. In Crystal's case, she had contained these festering feelings and images for years. She had organized her life around avoiding situations that might trigger these images. This is a very natural coping mechanism for the trauma survivor. It helps keep anxiety at a manageable level. Over time, like any cancer not attended to, these feelings will eat away at the very center of the person. The self-identity of the person gets warped. The trauma begins to define the essence of who he or she is. This negative self-image usually drives the survivor toward self-defeating and sabotaging behaviors. Moreover, the life of the trauma survivor becomes more and more isolated as he or she pursues systematic rituals of avoidance. Crystal's story is a classic unfolding of this universal dynamic that is present when one has been violated at a core level.

The hope is that at some juncture in time the survivor will fully awaken to an awareness of how these toxic feelings, behaviors, and cognitions are destroying the core of who he or she is and surrender to some help.

The story of the trauma survivor's journey has been likened to an exile during which a person feels alienated and disconnected from his or her very soul. There is no place within that he or she can call home;

no place within where he or she can sit back, take a deep breath, relax, and feel safe.

The story lived out in these pages is a dramatic account of one soul's process of awakening to its own sense of alienation and suffering. It is also a wonderful account of how transformation is the natural outcome of courageously facing suffering. From this perspective it is a Gospel story; a deeply Christian story. For it is in the messiness and pain of our lives (The Cross) that the Christian movement from death to life, takes on a very personal meaning. It has been a blessing for me in many ways to see how Crystal engaged this painful but transformative journey. This journey led her into the depths of her traumatic experience, and she eventually emerged with a whole new sense of self, the world, and God. This is a living example of what happens when one chooses to face the painful aspects of one's history.

This is Crystal's story, a story that chronicles her journey through the complex and arduous topography of grief, guilt, shame, fear and all those sticky feelings that cling to every survivor of child or adolescent sexual trauma. It also chronicles the processes involved in a healing and transformative journey as she begins to reclaim her life from the traumatic memory. The reader will see in these pages a vibrant spirituality unfolding out of what was once a wasteland.

But this is also a story of the resilient human spirit and how it refuses to be destroyed, how it will endlessly seek out light, hope, possibility, and all those aspects that truly make us fully human. The resilient nature of Crystal's story is an archetype of every human spirit's potential and propensity toward healing, growth, and wholeness.

As you engage in this story, you will discover that I am the one that happened to be the trigger for some very disturbing memories for Crystal; such triggers are never planned or controlled. I have been in a very privileged place since then, as Crystal has trusted me with the pain she carries regarding her traumatic experience. I have gotten to witness her awaken to this pain, work through the pain, and then come to a place at which she reached full resolution and reconciliation within herself and with all the characters in the story. For whatever reason you may have picked up this book, may it inspire you to believe again, to trust again that the spirit cannot be eternally shattered. The capacity to choose how to respond to and work with feelings and thoughts associated with sexual abuse is always beckoning one forward toward healing, growth, and a new self. Crystal's story is an embodiment of this spirit, with its innate human capacity to choose how to respond to the most disturbing of life's experiences.

Before I put down my pen, I need to point to another pain, another level of suffering in these pages. This pain is the pain the priest must have carried either consciously or unconsciously. This type of abuse could only come from a life overflowing with pain. This story sadly exposes a very dark and silent area of clerical and church life. The milieu of denial and suppression of sexuality within the institutional church culture helped create the conditions in which such abuse could become possible. The pain individual priests and clergy had to carry because of this denial remains one of the salient but silent themes in this book. I point to this because of my history. I am an ex-priest and went through seminary in this repressive environment. This book points to a church culture that did not have the capacity to help their young seminarians grow and develop into psychosexual maturity. This is indeed tragic, especially given that celibacy was to be essential to their lifestyle. Because celibacy is an essential aspect of a priest's lifestyle it is all the more vital that priests be given all the tools necessary to negotiate a healthy sense of their own sexuality.

It is through the courageous and altruistic voices like Crystal's that the church can be invited to ask the very difficult questions it has avoided down through the centuries. One's hope is that the hierarchy within the church can accept and engage stories like Crystal's and use these experiences to inform doctrine and policy pertaining to the psychosexual development of their seminarians. One might even stretch this and hope the church might feel compelled to engage in a radical new conversation about celibacy. The depth of experience in these pages has much wisdom to offer to a struggling institution; all one can hope for is that there are open and discerning hearts within the hierarchy courageous enough to take on board the full implications of this story. If there are such open hearts with an ability to listen deeply to this and many more stories like this, one can only imagine the wonderful possibilities for a new church to emerge with a new level of integrity.

Chapter 1: What If?

What would change in your world if your beloved priest or pastor became the target of sexual abuse allegations? Would you believe it? *Could* you believe it? What if the man you viewed as perfect and Christ-like had a hidden, secret life that only was revealed to young children or adolescents who didn't have the psychological finesse to see it as abusive or manipulative? Could you envision your spiritual leader methodically caressing a child's breast? I'm sure it is painful and shocking to contemplate how that would feel. Now imagine trying to live it. Try imaging that it is *you* lying on a bed, exposed in only your underwear and your beloved priest begins to narrate the details of your body. Can you bear the thought? What would you do? Not, what *should* you do... everyone knows the answer to that. If you knew everything this man had ever stood for was truth, compassion, and holiness, and yet, that was only a part of who he was, could you separate the two?

What if the Christ-like man wasn't just Christ-like to you, but to a whole parish, a whole community? How would you challenge an entire church to believe differently when all his actions and words were in direct conflict with the accusations against him?

Although I can't answer that question for you, it can shed some light into why so many victims of sexual abuse remain quiet well into their adult years, if not forever. The humiliation felt from the abuse is but a crumb compared to the humiliation of a congregation doubting your truth. What character flaw does the accuser have that makes it so difficult to believe? What character attribute does the priest have to be defended without hesitation?

If accusations of sexual abuse against a beloved priest were true and legitimate, would it take away from the good he brought to the world? I'm sure the infants baptized in the name of the Father, the Son, and the Holy Spirit aren't denied access to heaven because of his sexual sins. Does the sacrament of matrimony become null and void because a sexual predator performed it? The answer is of course 'no' because in those moments, Christ was acting through him to do His will. Just as one can be happy and angry during the same day, so too, I guess, could one be both gracious and sinful in the same day. If God touched all those who were blessed by this priest's actions through baptism and matrimony, does it then mean that I was cursed by his actions and brushed the face of Satan? How can it be possible to be condemned without even realizing that you are?

So often through this process I have felt the words of Christ as he died upon the cross, "My God, my God, why have you forsaken me?" But, then I am reminded of what was given to us in Ephesians, Chapter 2: "But because of his great love for us, God, who is rich in mercy, made us alive in Christ even when we were dead in transgressions—it is by grace you have been saved." I often find myself fluctuating somewhere between those two thoughts.

Easter morning 1974.

Chapter 2: Family of Origin

I was born into a Catholic-American family during a time when birth control was considered a sin. There really wasn't any such thing as family planning, so many couples in my parents' generation had large families whether they had the financial and emotional resources to nurture their children or not. Thus, I was the fifth child born to my parents, the little girl longed for after four boys. But by the time I entered this world, the first smile, first steps, first anything were not so new anymore.

I was deeply loved by my parents who provided me with the shelter, food, warmth, and education that I needed at great sacrifice to themselves. Even so, I somehow missed the feeling of being precious, wanted and loved more than anything in the world. My parents felt all those things in their hearts; but didn't communicate their love to me in a way that I understood. Consequently, I was a needy kid. I turned to the other adults in my life to meet my emotional needs. I was the teacher's pet, and all my energy and effort was focused on pleasing the grown-ups. I had friends; but they were my second option if a caring adult wasn't around. I remember never being content in the presence of my friends. I was always thinking of ways to gain the attention and approval of the chosen adults in my life. I was quite obsessive about it. I would think about it on my ride to school and at night I would retreat early to my bedroom to lie in bed and fantasize about how much concern they had for me. It was quite self-centered. I never really understood this insatiable need for approval from adults, but I always knew it wasn't normal.

Beginning in the third grade, I remember feeling anxious and unsettled. I knew something was not right, but could not identify or label it. It left me feeling that I was on the outside looking at everyone within. It made for a very long and sad childhood. It has taken me well into my thirties to understand that need, and even now on a bad day I could not explain it if I were asked to. I experience it much like understanding what a word means but not able to define it.

Most of the adults that I became attached to did not have abusive or selfish qualities. Most of them were teachers, and, although they weren't equipped with the education or experience to help me, they remained kind, supportive and ever-present. All of them were female, and as I look back, they were the bridges that kept me above water and helped me along my journey. They were my spiritual mothers... the rest of the village it took to raise this child. I will always look back fondly on our time together. I stay connected with most of them. We are now able to enjoy a true and equal friendship.

My mother has always been a strong presence in my life. She was a great person to share the day's events with, but I never felt comfortable sharing my unhappiness. I felt responsible for her success and happiness and it placed a great burden on me to shield her from my sadness. I could mask my melancholy the moment I walked in the door from school and never give any sign that anything was wrong, but when it was time to go to school, I allowed my gloom to surface. My mother never asked this of me, but I couldn't bear the guilt of exposing my sadness to her and feeling responsible for her disappointment. I couldn't carry the weight of both our regrets. As a result, I never allowed my mother to really know me. She knew a façade, a front that I put up to protect her. I revealed to her only the happy, positive moments in my life, and as a result, her perception of me was skewed. In some warped way, it expressed the volume of love in my heart for her, my precious mother.

I wanted her to feel proud of her parenting as I developed into a young lady. Because I had food, clothes, shelter and warmth, I couldn't find the words to share my pain. I couldn't tell her that all she gave wasn't enough. I needed more. I needed her to make sure I had a ride to and from athletics. I needed her to offer money for lunch instead of having to ask and feeling guilty because I knew money was short. I needed her to be my biggest cheerleader and attend all my extracurricular activities. And when the time came for my journey into therapy, I needed her unconditional support and the gift of space to work through what I didn't understand. I needed her to be emotionally available to hear me without unconsciously placing her feelings about how I was doing back in my lap. I did not need for her insecurity about my participation in therapy to spill over to me in the form of a guilt trip. I needed her to relax and let go of the "I'm a bad mother" complex.

She wasn't a bad mother. In fact, she was a very loving mother. Despite not giving me the needed emotional support, she did many things that I wouldn't trade for anything. To this day, I try to re-create them for my own daughters. For instance, when I was a child, not a night passed when she didn't rock me to sleep or scratch my back as I got older. She praised my academic abilities and successes. She cooked a warm, homemade meal each evening. How could she give so much, and yet in the end, never focus her unconditional attention on me?

My father was away from home for long periods. His employer required lengthy travel so he came home only on weekends, if then. Because of that, I have very few childhood memories of my father, and it has taken all these years finally to *know* him. I was afraid of him. His voice was loud even when he wasn't angry. There was never time to play. He was stern and short-tempered, yet always made sure I had all I needed. He never hesitated to give me the last dollar in his wallet, but it came with a big sigh, letting me know that supporting me financially was a strain. I know now that he did everything for us out of genuine love, but to me it never felt that way. Both my parents did the very best they could from what they knew. I am sure they attempted to correct their parents' mistakes; just as I will attempt to correct theirs. And, along the way, I am sure I will make new mistakes for my children to work on in their adult years.

My parents and both sets of grandparents were devout Catholics, strictly following Church law. I went to Mass faithfully on a weekly basis, attended CCD classes until my senior year, participated in the youth choir, served as an altar girl, etc. We sat down as a family each night and after church on Sundays to share a meal together after repeating the traditional Catholic blessing. My parents taught me that priests were an extension of God and were infallible.

Junior high began as an oasis in my emotional desert. I joined cheerleading, volleyball, basketball, track and band. I especially loved artistic roller-skating and started to compete in local and regional contests. Roller-skating would become my life-long passion. Back then, I had no idea what gifts and blessings this sport would bring to me. The summer between my eighth and ninth grade year, I dropped all extracurricular activities and focused on skating full time. I loved every minute when I was on skates. While skating, I wasn't hurting inside. It was my escape. Mornings started with happy anticipation of another day at the rink. My love for skating kept away any regrets about not pursuing other activities, other sports. I felt special and blessed. I could escape my sadness through strenuous physical effort. At a time when I could not yet verbalize my inner feelings, I could express them through physical movement, interpreting the music in harmony with them. My parents' support in introducing me to skating and encouraging me in it has been a life-long gift. I am forever grateful for their sacrifice.

Just as I entered ninth grade, my skating coach resigned from the program. My parents were as frustrated as I was, because this was the third coach I'd lost. Now, my mother had to travel two hours round trip every day to the rink and back. It is among the greatest gifts she ever gave me. The cost of skating amounted to several hundred dollars a month, so, reluctantly, we made the joint decision to withdraw from the skating program. Devastated and heart-broken, I was left with nothing but my schoolwork to occupy my mind.

It was too late to join the extracurricular activities at school, except for Pep Squad. Despite being a cheerleader in junior high school, Pep Squad held no interest for me, but I joined anyway, just to make a connection. Depression quickly smothered my desire for life and I grew stale inside as my soul became dormant. I could not respond to people's attempts to comfort me and became all the more depressed the farther I moved away from their cheeriness and joy. The people in my life could neither see nor hear me. Despair and depression darkened my life and made all activities equally sterile. I could not explain what was wrong, despite desperately wanting to. I became constantly embarrassed and ashamed of my mood and thoughts. During this time, my chest and neck took on a beet-red appearance for hours every day. I became so self-conscious about the outward display of my inner anxiety that I altered my wardrobe. I would only wear clothes that covered my chest and neck. Typically, teenagers wear as little as possible. Now, not only did I stand out because of my moodiness and withdrawal, but my choice of clothes isolated me even more. I shrank inside and no one noticed.

Chapter 3: The Downward Spiral

My brothers had grown up and left home with lives of their own. My father worked in Boston at the time and I saw him at most once a month. My mother worked nights and went to college in the evenings. When I got home from school, she was off to college and then to work. I ate dinner alone; completed homework alone; watched television alone, and finally went to bed in an empty, echoing house. I was essentially living on my own at age fifteen. My mom came back from work just as I left for school, and we often waved to each other as we passed on the road. I was lonely and often frightened in that big house out in the country.

Home alone one evening, I was studying in the family room. A wall separated our family room from the formal living room. A set of ceramic wind chimes hung from the ceiling in the living room. I would sometimes forget the chimes hanging there and run into them. They were low enough that my head hit them with a loud crash, reminding me of dishes breaking.

Childhood home

View outside my childhood bedroom window

That night, all was quiet in the house. The radio and television were not on. We were rural enough that there was no street noise.

Suddenly, the wind chimes rang as though someone had accidentally walked into them. My heart pounded in my throat. An intruder must be in the house! I started toward the living room, but stopped halfway, instead retreating to the kitchen. I grabbed a butcher knife. I couldn't bring myself to go see what might have hit the chimes. I left the house and walked down the road with the knife gripped tightly in my hand. The road was gravel, I was barefoot, it was winter, and I wore only thin pajamas.

The neighborhood was divided into three-to-five acre lots with a great deal of space between each house. The lots on either side of my parent's home and across the street were vacant. There were no streetlights and the moon was not out. It was pitch black. My heart pounded in my chest and drummed in my ears. Someone was in my house! Coyotes howled in the distance and, in the empty lot next door, brush rustled as deer scampered away. Panting in fear, I stayed outside for several hours, too afraid of the dark and the noises to walk to the neighbors', too terrified to return to the house and the intruder.

At last, I did go back and summoned the courage to go through the entire house searching under the beds and in the closets, making sure there was no stranger there. By that time it was well past midnight. I was exhausted. I climbed into bed and just as I rested my head on the pillow, the phone rang. Again, my heart in my throat, I raced to answer. No one responded to my "hello." I collapsed on the floor and sobbed myself to sleep, realizing I was not in control.

The neighborhood where I grew up was so isolated that 911 services were not available. Even if they had been, I could only have said, "Please, send someone; I'm scared." How silly that would have appeared! But that experience made it clear I did not feel cared for or protected. Instead, I felt completely abandoned… by my parents and my God.

During that ordeal, my father was out-of-town once again; my brothers busy with wives and lives of their own. I never once considered calling my mother and telling her I was frightened. I thought my mother would dismiss my fears as insignificant, unfounded and silly. What I wanted above all things but didn't have the emotional sophistication to realize, was to call my mother to tell her I was frightened and for her to reply, "Don't worry; I'm on my way home right now. You are safe." I wanted my mother to intuit my need without spelling it out for her. Perhaps she would have responded just that way had I given her the chance, but even so, I would have been racked with guilt for causing her to leave her job in the middle of the shift.

The next morning, I awoke in a fog, exhausted physically and mentally. Stunned from the trauma of the night, I dressed and went to school. Only when I stood at my locker before my first class did I realize that my fist was still locked around the butcher knife I had pulled from the kitchen drawer the night before. Startled and embarrassed, I slipped the large blade behind the textbooks in my locker. I went about my day, numb and detached, until a voice from an overhead speaker called my name. I was to report to the office. Indifferent and despondent, I made my way to the front of the building where the Mrs. Winn, the high school counselor and the principle met me.

This meeting was a turning point. Mrs. Winn revealed herself as one of the most loving and compassionate persons I have known. Here began a long, turbulent relationship, yet a rewarding and fulfilling one. She became the 'spiritual mother' who guided me through the labyrinth of high school. She remained kind, non-judgmental and supportive. I relied on her for the backing and encouragement that she gave generously, without making me feel guilty or wanting anything in return. She was a kind, precious lady and I grew to adore her. She had an amazing level of tolerance for my behavior and empathy for what I was feeling. I didn't make it easy for her. Each day I presented her with a new, histrionic trauma. It never stopped. By now, I see that I feared she would abandon me and my excessive needs, and so I daily tested her support and acceptance with my histrionics. No matter how much patience, empathy and approval she offered, I was never satisfied. I understood that my need could not be filled, which only added to my depression and shame. I grew dependent on Mrs. Winn in a sick and desperate way, and I hated that because I loved and admired her. Looking back on those high school years, I see that Mrs. Winn's dedication to me kept suicide at bay during the years we shared together. I loved her then and still do to this day. She even honored me by acting as one of my bridesmaids at my wedding.

The student who had the locker beneath mine discovered the knife that had slipped down the back of the locker. Only the blade was visible. He quickly reported the knife to Mrs. Winn. The principal, irritated from the outset, asked what I thought I was doing with a knife at school. He had a preconceived idea of my purpose, and my explanation must have sounded like Charlie Brown's teacher: "wah-wah-wah-wah." Any attempt to communicate proved pointless. That moment branded me as troubled and misunderstood. Throughout the next four years of high school, I didn't disappoint. I was troubled and misunderstood. As the years went by, my behavior grew more and more disturbing, odd, and unpredictable. I became expert at creating false dramas to communicate the unhappiness I was unable to verbalize.

The principal escorted me to my locker and requested that I open it. I wasn't even concerned about the knife inside. Violence was unheard of in our school and I had no idea what he was thinking. He confiscated the knife, walked me back to the office and summoned my mother for a conference. She was baffled, embarrassed and altogether irritated, but defended my reputation and contested the severity of the problem. This was her first hint that something was wrong. I received a five-day suspension from school and a reluctant commitment from my mother to provide psychological counseling for me. The five-day suspension was designed to be punishment for bringing a knife to school, but for me it was worse. It allowed my depression and suicidal thoughts to flourish without restraint. The suspension isolated me even further. This seminal event had a snowball effect that placed me in the hands of my greatest comforter, but the one who injured me the most.

My mother honored her commitment to provide counseling for me, although she never wholly accepted the idea of psychotherapy. Her concern focused on her overwhelming fear that she was a bad mother, and the school and the therapist would recognize that and blame her. She never coached me on what to say in therapy, but I always dreaded the end of a session, because I knew my mother would question me about what was discussed. Therefore, I didn't feel I had the space or privacy to discuss the issues. I had little trust in my therapist and did not know that the information shared would not be given to my mother without my permission. My mother did pressure my therapist to reveal the content of our discussions. There were pros and cons to this situation. My therapist created a safe environment for me to process feelings and events, but my mother, who was paying the bill, never trusted my therapist's abilities or motives. Years passed while nothing was accomplished because of this conflict. Not until I could pay the therapist myself did I feel free to talk. Once in college, sessions were based on my need, without my mother's knowledge, and were paid from my part-time salary. They were expensive, but freedom always is. There would be no one waiting at the end of each visit to inquire about our conversations.

Chapter 4: My Greatest Comforter, My Greatest Injury

At the beginning of my freshman year in high school, my family's parish held a mission. We rarely had a guest priest come to our church, since we were a tiny community in a rural area. Father Michael was a dynamic and engaging speaker. A man in his late forties, his striking eyes, blue with long, straight eyelashes, captured everyone's attention and we held our collective breath for his next words. He was funny, and spoke of real world issues—everyone could relate to him.

On the last night of the mission, several priests attended and offered the Sacrament of Reconciliation. This was a new experience for me, as our parish did not offer individual confession unless specifically requested. I was not raised with that version of the Sacrament as part of my religion. We were absolved of our sins as a congregation—that was all I knew. I was very interested in participating in this Sacrament, for something lay heavy on my heart that I wanted to confess, but never before had the courage to admit. The week of the mission had given me strength, and I sought out Father Micheal to hear my confession because I felt he was compassionate and would not pass judgment. That single fifteen-minute conversation with him would change the course of my life.

I was right; he was very compassionate. From that moment, he became my friend, my mentor, my parent. I grew to love him deeply. I trusted him with everything I had, for he carried my secret and loved me anyway. When he looked at me, I thought his eyes were filled with compassion. Now, in hindsight, I know it was only lust… but I was too young to understand what lust was. Years of sexual abuse were ahead for me, but I had no way of knowing.

Before this priest came to my parish, I was deeply depressed. I could not explain the origin of my depression because I did not know myself. During a visit with a teacher one day, the conversation led her to assume that I had been raped. She suggested that, and I did not correct her. This was my secret: a lie about a rape that never occurred. I could never bring myself to correct her because it seemed like something tangible that would explain why I was so depressed and suicidal. That secret became Father Michael's power over me because he knew if I confessed I'd been lying about the rape and then accused him of sexual abuse, no one would believe me.

As my relationship with Father Michael developed and my depression and suicidal tendencies increased, my mother would bring me to the rectory to visit with him. She would wait in the car, reading a book during our sessions. I can remember staring out the window at her, in a daze, feeling completely empty inside.

Father Michael often drove his old, red Dodge pick-up truck to my parents' home to go swimming with me. My father was working in a different state during this time and my mother worked nights and slept during the day. Both were aware of his visits, but thought nothing of it. They were relieved to know someone would be there while I was swimming in case of an accident. Of course, those were the pre-scandal days when sexual abuse in the Catholic Church wasn't uppermost in everyone's mind. It wasn't even on the radar. Swimming with him was fun. I would stand on his shoulders and flip off into the deep end. It all seemed innocent fun and even now, I'm not sure it wasn't. Yet an uncomfortable closeness developed. I don't remember any molestation in the pool, but I do remember a lot of climbing, jumping, wrestling and splashing. Maybe that was when the thoughts first came into his mind.

Once, a friend from school was swimming with us. She was Catholic and had met him during the same mission I had. They excused themselves and went around to the front sidewalk. Darcy had something to confess. My internal warning system went off, but I didn't know exactly why. Darcy was extremely promiscuous and I was concerned for her, but at the same time, I didn't want to know. I respected their privacy and we never discussed it. I have often thought about that day. I haven't spoken with Darcy since high school, but several times I have considered finding her and asking exactly what happened.

The manipulation and abuse was subtle. For the first time, I internally questioned whether something was not right when I was about to leave one of our 'visits.' He hugged me, but when I tried to release, he continued to hold me. I remember thinking, *how strange*. On the next visit he began a new custom: to give me a gentle kiss on the cheek as he hugged me good-bye. This always felt awkward, but I was too insecure to comment. I would just fidget my way out of the room. The kiss on the cheek led to kissing my neck, and I can still smell the stale alcohol on his breath. I was always self-conscious. How do you respond to something like that? Mostly, I ignored it and pretended it wasn't happening. I remember trying to act nonchalant. All the while, my face, neck and chest bloomed with red welts from anxiety. Even though my gut told me something was wrong, I ignored it because he filled my need for compassion, to be considered worthy, to be accepted. Those needs were not met in my home. My survival depended on meeting those needs, no matter the cost. How does one confront a priest, a man of God, about inappropriate behavior—especially, when one is young, inexperienced and naïve?

The rectory where Father Michael lived had two stories. The downstairs functioned as the business area, with several offices and secretaries. He lived there throughout what I called the 'grooming years'—the early years of our time together. There were two offices downstairs, which we often used. The first one was cluttered with church items. It was more of a storage room than an office, but there was a door that provided privacy, so it was sufficient. The items in the room were of particular importance, because there were statues of the Virgin Mary as well as other saints. The visual impact of these images blended with the subtlety of his actions began the collision between religion and sexual abuse. That first prolonged embrace that wouldn't release happened in this office. A specter still dwells in that room: the ghost of my first inkling that something was wrong. My guilt shares the room with the ghost because I chose to ignore what it was trying to tell me. God was whispering his warnings and I missed the message.

The second office, located at the opposite end of the building, was only used once, but its walls witnessed the moment when a priest chose sin over grace. I'm sure it was not God's voice that spoke to him that day and urged him on. Or, maybe God was speaking to him, but he chose to ignore those whispers in his heart. This office had a leather sofa which I'm sure was used by many parishioners to share their woes with an understanding and forgiving priest. But, I wonder if those parishioners would have been as open to sharing if they had known the secrets the sofa held. As Father Michael and I entered the office, he collapsed on the sofa, claiming he was exhausted from all his travels. Had he stopped there, it would have shown his humanity without the sin. However, his next action left me speechless, with the awkward fidgetiness I described earlier. He grabbed my wrist and pulled me on top of him so that we were lying face to face. It was so unexpected that I couldn't process his action quickly enough to react, so I pretended we were both just sitting in separate chairs talking, and responded as if we were. There was no discussion of his actions. His hands caressed my body, but not in a blatantly sexual way. Confused, unable to understand what was happening, I stood up and ran out of the office. He caught up with me outside and gently scolded me. Shame on me! What would the secretaries out front think about my hasty exit? In the years that followed, I never ran out again.

When the two downstairs offices no longer provided the privacy he was seeking, he took me upstairs to the priests' private living quarters. This was taboo, because no one was ever allowed in their private living quarters. It was clean, even sterile. There were religious pictures on the walls as well as the ever-present crucifix… the constant reminder that God is watching. None of the other residents were present that day; so I was invited into their common living room.

It wasn't the most inviting room I'd seen; rather, it seemed cold and unwelcoming. No family pictures hung on the wall or anything else that expressed personal taste. It was all very 'generic.' For the first time, I understood that a priest's life might be filled with sadness and loneliness. My amazed attention focused on the wet bar, stocked with each resident's favorite liquor. Father Michael preferred scotch and water. Not only did he pour himself a drink, but offered me one as well. It was my first taste of alcohol. To this day I reject alcohol because of that memory. He sat in a recliner. The dark paneling and closed blinds darkened the room and increased its gloom. The only light was directly over the wet bar.

Again, Father Michael grabbed my wrist and pulled me into his lap. He started rocking and I completely zoned out. I remember staring through a hole in the blinds, out the window, across the street at the doorknob of a nearby home. That was my focal point and I didn't dare look away. Years later, as a hospice nurse, I knocked on that same door to admit the man of the house to hospice. It was a surreal moment and I took some time to gather myself before putting on my professional hat and entering their home to begin a journey that for them would be even more devastating. In my time with Father Michael I would stare at the doorknob and wonder what the people were like inside. Were they retired? Did they have children? Grandkids? How was their house decorated? What did they do for fun? What were they cooking for supper that night? Anything to escape the present moment.

I cannot recall how that visit ended. I don't remember walking down the stairs; I don't remember leaving in the car; I don't remember if I was crying or acting nonchalant. I just don't remember. These lapses of memory deeply concern me. What else don't I remember?

Finally, I could no longer tolerate his actions, and at age sixteen I decided to confront him. I was too afraid to talk directly with him, so I wrote him a letter. We agreed to meet at a local diner to discuss it. I was nervous because this was my first time to drive alone and I knew I was not equipped to steer the confrontation I was about to have. After lunch, I handed him the letter. He read it… and just chuckled. The second most devastating moment of my life was coming.

He looked up at me and said, "Silly little girl! Why would you ever think anything like that? I could never do anything to hurt you. I am so embarrassed!"

That was the end of the conversation. I left feeling mortified that I had accused a priest of sexual misconduct that never happened. Only, it did happen. I never questioned his actions again.

The next time I saw Father Michael, I was particularly despondent. My anxiety about my relationship with him was mounting but I didn't have the sophistication or confidence to know what to do.

He looked at me with a smile and said, "I know what you exactly what you need."

He arranged a dinner with one of his "other friends." Her name was Dana, a young woman of twenty or twenty-one, but she seemed much older to me. She had an apartment of her own within walking distance of Father Michael's living quarters. There was no explanation how they met or what was their relationship, and I didn't dare ask. The three of us prepared a casual dinner. Father Michael made the best mashed potatoes I have ever tasted, and to this day, I judge every mashed potato against his. He popped a Sara Lee pie in the oven, and I remember his jovial remark that Sara Lee had taught him to bake. Superficially, it was an enjoyable meal with good company, but underneath lay awkwardness that could not be seen or explained. Earlier, on the way to her apartment, Father Michael had hinted that Dana's life experiences mirrored my own and she was doing well now. He felt that meeting her would ease the anxiety in my heart.

During our visit, the conversation never drifted toward our life histories, but the unspoken communication spoke volumes. It was as if there was a silent understanding that Dana and I were caught in the same trap that neither of us could escape. Like two flies caught in a web, we stared at each other, wondering how we got there. That was my only meeting with Dana and to this day I think of her and wonder whether the relationship with Father Michael left her as broken as I was. A haunting memory of that meeting still lingers.

Chapter 5: *Why am I so Broken?*

As the severity of the abuse increased throughout the high school years, so did the desperate ways I chose to act out my anxiety. My sophomore and junior years were fairly quiet and I had successfully made it through the Varsity Cheerleading tryouts. Cheerleading proved to be a great distraction for me. It provided the structure needed to withstand the extreme anxiety stirring in me, but as my senior year approached, I found it difficult to maintain the façade of the perky little cheerleader. I struggled just to go to school, and once there, became disengaged and disinterested in my classes. Despite having been academically successful in years past, I now resorted to cheating on homework assignments because I didn't have the emotional energy to complete them the night before. Weeks had passed since I had paid attention in class, so I hadn't absorbed the knowledge to complete the coursework. Every day I fought to keep my head above water.

Just as my senior year in high school began and right in the middle of football season, I dropped out of cheerleading. This decision would haunt me for years to come. Dropping out of cheerleading left me

Varsity Cheerleading, 1988

without the focus I so desperately needed. My anguish grew. Father Michael became more refined and audacious in his quest for sexual gratification. I was within months of the breaking point.

Without cheerleading, the evenings became void of activity. Surely, that simple act of dropping cheerleading should have sounded an alarm that something wasn't right, but my decision never raised an eyebrow or sparked a question, at least not in my presence. I now spent my evenings at home alone with my thoughts. Those thoughts spiraled around two themes: how I could I explain to Mrs. Winn that I had been lying to her for four years about such a horrible subject as rape and at the same time explain that a priest was using me for sexual pleasure? I could never find a solution. The second theme was my suicide and the insignificance of my life.

The abuse continued and worsened with each visit. Until one day, when I was a senior in high school, I walked out of my English class to use the restroom but instead got into my car and drove to the Gulf Coast. I didn't remember the drive. The Gulf Coast in that region is not beautiful, but there I felt closest to God. Any large body of water has a way of drawing me closer to God because the sheer size makes me realize that something larger than myself is in control.

At the bay, I sat on the sea wall, staring at the water for hours in a blank daze. I was in an indescribable emotional state. I wasn't crying. I wasn't conjuring up ways to be self-destructive. I was empty of all emotion. I was aware of my surroundings, but everything seemed blurred and muffled. Despondent and indifferent would be the best way to describe my emotional state. I did not know how to escape the relentless pain I was in. Depression had wrapped itself around my spirit so tightly that I was indifferent to all feeling. Surely, this wasn't what God intended my life to be! Hours went by. Hunger came and went. I was frozen in despair with no one competent enough to grasp that I did not understand my own emotional state. My behavior was as complex and confusing to me as it was to everyone else. I kept asking myself, "Why am I so broken?"

Exhausted and weary, I made my way to the one place where I could find solace… the church. I sat in the empty cathedral sobbing, not knowing what to do. The church was a place of peace that always drew me, yet it was haunted with the secrets I kept for it. The priest of that parish provided a hotel room and an evening meal for me before I returned home the next day.

That incident landed me in a psychiatric hospital for the rest of my senior year. During those eight months, I struggled. I wanted to die; I wanted help; I wanted to punish myself; I wanted to escape. I could not escape and it was a good thing because that hospital and the people working there truly saved my life. They gave me the space and the support I needed to confront my demons… except sexual abuse by a priest. Once I had come clean in therapy about the false rape, how could I then turn around and tell everyone that a priest was sexually abusing me? I was stuck.

Father Michael's kind and encouraging words had prompted me to confess the lie about the rape. By the time I had reached my senior year in high school, the story of the rape had grown to enormous proportions with many details. I had made the story real to me and everyone I shared it with. I lived a lie daily, and it consumed every fiber of my being. Father Michael consistently and lovingly encouraged me to let go of the lie and assured me that Mrs. Winn, in whom I had placed all my hope, trust and admiration, would accept my confession and still support me without question. His was good and kind advice, but he also knew that should I choose to confess my dramatic lie publicly, his own secret with me would be safe. Who could possibly believe my story that a priest was living out his sexual fantasies with me when I had just confessed a four year, extensive, detailed lie about a rape that never happened? Father Michael surely knew he had total freedom to use me as he saw fit with no one to challenge his actions. His was the greatest violation of all. I confessed my lie to him during the Sacrament of Reconciliation, Confession. That Father Michael should use this holy Sacrament as a means to indulge his sexual fantasies is a travesty, a sacrilege, a betrayal of sacrosanct ecclesiastical tenets, not to mention betrayal of one young girl's trust.

A patient in a mental hospital takes on an alien identity. Although we in the United States of America pride ourselves on our liberties, there I instantly lost the most basic freedoms. Imagine for a minute that you must follow a schedule not of your choosing: told when to eat, when to sleep and when to use the restroom. Participation in therapy was non-negotiable. Imagine needing a breath of fresh air only to find the doors locked. Fresh air was only allowed under the watchful eye of the staff. My daily walks by myself were denied me. I suffered from extreme culture shock.

Upon admission, the staff inventoried my belongings, another indication that all privacy was lost. Not only did they inventory everything, they also removed what was considered 'contraband.' These items ranged from belts to glass makeup bottles to mirrors found in compacts to candy. Music and television were not allowed and soft drinks were not available. Any hygienic products were kept in a basket locked in a closet. You were told when you could access them. Eating utensils were plastic and ineffective. The knives broke as you tried to cut your food, but a real knife was considered too risky. Phone calls were not permitted except at certain times from a list of 'approved' callers. Remember, I was a teenager at the time and those restrictions felt like death. The day I was admitted, I was despondent, but curious and hopeful.

The next morning, the enormity of all I had lost struck me like a bomb and I was miserable. I felt like a caged animal. But despite the culture shock, over time I grew to love the predictability of the routine. Removed from all that was familiar, I was able to look inward. I could allow myself to feel without fear of rejection or reprimand. But this new experience, like all new experiences, brought on an anxiety attack. Thank God, I was surrounded by a staff of warm, caring people who did not judge. They supported me when I wasn't worthy of support and in a way that no one in my previous life could. As a result, I was able to 'get real' for the first time.

My stay at the hospital was short, maybe a month or two, and I was discharged home. But the stay was not long enough to unravel my complex emotional difficulties. Any hope I had gained faded when I returned to school. The air was filled with whispers of gossip and lack of understanding. I couldn't bear the judgmental looks as I passed by. No one dared to approach me. Once the school day was over, I returned home to lonely evenings with nothing to occupy my mind. I prayed out loud for help, and, not sensing an answer or a presence, I swallowed a half a bottle of Medrin, a prescription for my migraines. It was a half-hearted attempt to end my life, but in retrospect, it was really a cry for attention.

Out of fear, I induced vomiting to purge the medication from my system, but also called Mrs. Winn and Dr. Macey, my psychologist, for help. Both seemed irritated and frustrated, but both responded. Mrs. Winn, along with another teacher, arrived to ensure my safety. By coincidence, my youngest brother, five years older than me, came home during their visit, confused by Mrs. Winn's and the other teacher's presence. Once they were confident that my older brother would assume responsibility for me, they left, and I felt abandoned once more. Dr. Macey had instructed my brother to drive me to the nearest hospital for medical treatment, which he did. I was given charcoal to swallow to neutralize any remaining drug in my system. Charcoal has a miserable taste. Thick and dry, it leaves the teeth and mouth black. The remedy was a punishment in itself, which left an unpleasant enough impression that I would never choose to overdose again. I did not realize that the *real* punishment would come the next day in the form of violent, explosive diarrhea.

My mother was not present in the emergency room with me, nor did she arrive at the psychiatric hospital that night. I don't know why. I can't remember where she could have been. Perhaps at school and in the middle of final exams. Perhaps she was visiting my father who was working out-of-town. Perhaps she was working. I just can't remember and the subject is so emotionally charged that I can't ask her.

Once I was discharged and medically cleared from the emergency room, my brother drove me to the psychiatric hospital, what I had wanted all along. I felt safe and accepted there where my behavior was not considered unusual. The other patients welcomed me with open arms, and I felt relieved to be back.

The hospital staff never intended to keep me as long as I stayed or to keep me on an acute care unit long after the maximum of thirty days had passed. But my emotional state was so critical that they couldn't stabilize me enough to transfer me to an intermediate or long-term care unit or discharge me. I spent much of my time on the acute care unit under one-to-one supervision. My suicidal tendencies increased as therapy evolved, and although the thirty days passed, I continued to be a danger to myself. On many nights a mental health worker sat at my bedside as I slept. The staff member assigned to 'one-to-one' could be no farther than arm's length away at any time, including while I slept, showered, and used the restroom. It left no privacy. The staff was fighting for my life, and I took every opportunity to try to end it.

The staff made several attempts during my hospitalization to discharge me. At one point, they allowed me to attend my regular high school for a few hours in an attempt to ease me back and give the other kids a chance to get comfortable around me again. I was to sit in the classes and observe, to be present, no more. I chose to attend my Government class because I thought my Government teacher was kind-hearted and it would be an easy transition. He was not informed that I would be present that day and had planned to show the documentary "48 Hours in a Psychiatric Hospital." When the tape began to play, I collapsed in tears. I sobbed with my head on my desk, humiliated and devastated as class ended and my fellow students filed past on their way to lunch. The teacher, realizing the impact of the video, could only apologize with his eyes. He knew there were no words.

I returned to the hospital and begged them not discharge me. I was clear in my plea. I assured them that I would kill myself without fail on the first opportunity if they chose to let me go. It was a pivotal point for me. I had not yet confessed the story of the false rape and had relied upon it to explain my depression. With desperation, or perhaps, with strength never felt before, I sat before my psychiatrist, my psychologist, Lisa, the unit manager, and the nurses on the unit and poured my heart and soul out to them. I explained that I had made up the story about the rape because I was so depressed and suicidal, yet couldn't explain why. In giving up that story I was left with "I don't know what is wrong with me." I didn't speak of Father Michael's sexual abuse because I knew the wildest movie script couldn't match my life. I just wasn't believable.

When I left that meeting, I also left my fate in their hands. For the first time, they saw me nakedly honest. They had doubted the authenticity of the rape all along and were waiting for me to understand what it meant to *work* in therapy. I finally understood. My discharge only came some seven months after that conversation, when I began to understand and process the reasons behind the depression.

Kristin

During my hospitalization, I experienced, almost for the first time, a sense of 'belonging' among my peers. The behavior that caused me to not fit in was common among the other young people on the unit. We all had different histories, different families, but we all were there because we couldn't cope with what life had dealt us. I made great friends there. I could connect with them on a level that was not possible with my friends at school. One girl in particular had a profound influence on my life. Kristin. Like me, Kristin was suicidal and a very real attempt had brought her to the hospital. She had a tracheostomy as a result of a medication overdose. She was frail and her skin often appeared gray. Nobody could have known her misery. Despite all that, she remained pleasant and kind. There was a light in her eyes that even the deepest depression could not hide. Late at night, when all the other kids were asleep and the staff was busy doing whatever they did when we slept, Kristin and I would sneak into each other's rooms and stay up for hours talking. Several times the staff broke up our nightly meetings, but most of the time they made us hot chocolate and kept our late night girl talks to themselves. Kristin and I became great friends. She was self-conscious about her tracheostomy and was disillusioned that her attempt had such devastating results. I wish I'd had the insight then to sense her impending death.

When graduation day came for my high school class, Kristin was struggling to decide whether to leave the hospital or stay. She decided to leave, because she knew she wasn't doing the necessary work and was worried about the financial burden for her mother. So, she was discharged. That weekend, I was out on pass to attend my high school graduation. Kristin was to spend the night with me… but she never came. When I returned to the psychiatric hospital on Sunday evening, Lisa, the unit manager, came to the hospital. That was extremely rare because she worked Monday through Friday and was *never* seen on weekends. She had come in to talk with me. I knew something important had happened. We sat on my bed and she explained that Kristin had taken an overdose of Tegretol and had lain down beside her mother. Her mother awoke when she heard Kristin's labored and slow breaths through her tracheostomy. She was pronounced dead on arrival at the hospital. I remember crying, but it was forced mourning. I knew that was the appropriate response, but I really didn't feel grief—at least not initially. My first thoughts were, *good for you girl,* for I had known the anguish in her heart. There were even feelings of jealousy that she had succeeded and I had not.

The next morning, Lisa again came to my room. I could see that her heart was burdened as she searched for words. She explained that when the nurses returned to Kristin's room to complete the post-mortem care, they found a heartbeat. She remained on life support for two days before dying. Once again, hours later, in came Lisa to inform me of her death. This time, my grief was real, for I had seen the pain in everyone's eyes. In the hospital, boundaries were respected and obeyed without question, but on this occasion, every staff member collapsed in grief. They were struggling with her death as much as I was. I was overwhelmed. I just wanted to be unconscious so I picked up a hard-soled shoe and began beating my face and head in an attempt to knock myself unconscious. Four to five staff members restrained me and gave me Thorazine. They placed me in four-point leather restraints where I remained for the next eight hours. First, Kristin was alive… then she was dead… then she was alive… then she was dead. I kept waiting for the next piece in the sequence that never came. I was grateful for the Thorazine because I truly wanted a 'time-out' from my life.

Several days later, the staff decided it would help me to attend her memorial service. Lisa and Hannah, a mental health worker, escorted me there. It was very difficult to face Kristin's mother. Her grief permeated the church and squeezed all the oxygen out of the room. Lisa held me tight; she was unsure and fearful of my reaction. It was uninhibited grief. I realized there would be no more late night girl talks with my friend. My friend was gone.

Even now, years later, Kristin's death stays with me in the most powerful way. In moments of anguish when my thoughts turn toward suicide, I remember Kristin… and her mother. I often wonder what kind of woman she would have grown to be. What would her career choice have been? Children? To this day, I grieve over her death and hold her memory close to my heart.

Self Abuse-Self Release

Using a hard object to beat my face with was not a new coping skill I learned in the hospital. The first time I can recall doing this was in the third grade. I was taking a walk down the gravel road from my house. Sadness filled my being but I didn't understand why. Instinctively, I picked up a large rock and started to hit the right side of my face with a consistent, firm, repetitive motion. The pain was startling, but I discovered that it provided an immediate release of tension. The physical pain proved to be a distraction from the more confusing emotional pain. The coping mechanism, sick as it was, allowed me to survive through those years when I much rather would have been dead.

The self-abuse often left my face swollen and bruised. I became adept at creating plausible reasons why my face showed recurring trauma. Once I started roller-skating, it became easy because learning jumps and spins led to frequent falls. Skating left me with daily bruises, and I would invite anyone who questioned the cause of the bruises on my face to one of my skating practices. They felt reassured that the bruises came from athletic training and not from abuse. No one ever dreamed they were self-inflicted.

In the hospital, since I was under staff scrutiny at all times on a locked unit, it was only a matter of time before my self-abuse erupted. Once exposed, it seemed less important to hide it, and as therapy intensified and the pressure became unbearable, hitting my face became an instant release. At one point, I was even placed on 'shoe restriction' in an attempt to remove anything I could use to injure myself. I was out of control in my sadness and despair, so walls, floors, fists, and furniture became weapons against myself. I was filled with self-loathing and saw no possible recovery. I wasn't sure I would make it. Today, safely through all that pain, I see that not only did I make it, I have developed profound empathy for people who make wrong decisions and use ineffective and destructive coping skills. I understand their position and the thoughts behind those decisions. I know now that all choices are attempts to meet a need.

Hannah

Many professional, effective, and responsible staff members worked with me during my hospitalization, but a few could have used therapy themselves. I introduce Hannah because her blunders and errors in judgment taught me much. Painful lessons, but valuable. All the young people on the unit liked her. She was fun, insightful and also well liked by her peers. She worked the evening shift, far from the scrutiny and politics of the day shift. She became interested in me in the most peculiar way. I found her neutral; I didn't dislike her, but she also was not a person I would choose to confide in. Every evening, close to bedtime, she would bring all her charts into my room. She would work on her documentation as I was preparing for bed. We would talk a lot, but mostly about her struggles and demons. She would discuss the personal lives of the other staff members and let me read my own chart; I never objected. At the end of the day, I was mentally exhausted and talked-out, so I often had no more to contribute than a listening ear. She took full advantage of it and before I knew it, the roles were reversed. She was the patient and I the therapist. Every evening her thoughts became sicker. She desperately wanted me to be discharged from the hospital so that we could park my car in her garage with it running and die together. Hannah proposed the idea to cut the vacuum-cleaner hose and stick it into my exhaust pipe. Because I, too, had such a strong death wish, her idea sounded comforting and frightening at the same time. As the date for my discharge grew closer, my anxiety about leaving the hospital grew to enormous proportions. If I was discharged, I would not be strong enough to resist her plan. I even joked with Lisa about pitching a tent just outside the unit because I was trying not to leave. Of course, the staff and doctors had no hint of the source of my anxiety. I tried everything imaginable to postpone my discharge and when I realized nothing was going to work, I felt hopeless once again. My fate was decided; I would enter into her plan because nothing else could ease my relentless pain.

One Sunday, she was in my room. With her unit keys, she began to cut her flesh, starting just below the elbow on the inside of her arm. She had confessed doing this many times before, but had never abused herself in my presence. She wore long-sleeved clothing to hide the marks.

As she tore into her skin she said, "Ahh, screw it; I can't wait for you. I'm doing it tonight."

She left my room and continued her unit duties. Dr. Macey, my psychologist, walked in before I'd had time to take a breath. Typically, I would never have confided in her first. I would have practiced on other people before having the nerve to reveal something of this magnitude, but I was so unnerved by Hannah's actions that I found myself spilling all the months of conversations and behaviors to her. I didn't stop to think of the consequences. At that point, I would gladly have told the janitor. I had no idea of the enormity of the problem. I was numb from shock and fearful that she would kill herself. I was the only one who knew in advance of her plan.

What followed was equally shocking and difficult to absorb. Dr. Macey excused herself from my room for a short while. She came back, pulled up a chair and stayed to make sure Hannah would have no access to me for the rest of the day. Her action amazed me. I began to see her strong character. She sat with me all afternoon and until late in the evening while I wondered what she had planned for her evening and what she had sacrificed for me. Together, we walked to the administration building and notified Lisa. As the unit manager, it would be Lisa's responsibility to address this issue.

Hannah was removed from her job and taken away for her own treatment. I have never spoken with her again, but have heard through the grapevine that she remains in the same condition as the day she left my life. I often pray that she finds peace. I understand the turmoil she feels.

Humor Therapy

Not all of my time at the hospital was filled with sadness and despair. It was a great place that often felt more like a luxury camp than a mental hospital. When you fill a building with a bunch of unpredictable teenagers, anything can happen. Frequently, all the kids would be sent to their rooms in order to maintain confidentiality during periods when a particular individual needed some extra attention from the staff because of behavior problems. Those 'confidentiality breaks' could sometimes last a long time. Entertainment was hard to find, and I discovered just how creative my roommate and I could be in these quiet moments. We would tear open boxes of tampons and create beautiful flower arrangements. Remember, there was no television, music, or books. We would clog the wheel-chair accessible showers with towels and flood the bathroom just to splash in the water. Occasionally, we would witness some of the drama unfold before we were rushed to our room. There was one kid who was extremely obese and had the emotional maturity of a four-year old. He was annoying, even pathetic, but you couldn't help but like him. His histrionics provided great comedy relief. One time he became agitated when the nurse would not allow him a snack. He became angry, desperate. He ran into the unit kitchen and picked up the pot of hot coffee and proceeded to chase the nurse, who was very short and morbidly obese as well, around the room. The danger of physical harm was real, but it was a hilarious scene to watch: two short, fat people running around the unit, chasing each other. Even though they were out of breath, they continued to yell at each other. In that moment, it was impossible to tell who was the patient and who was the nurse, because both were equally ridiculous. Oh, the stories I could tell! An entire movie could be created around the different personalities enclosed in that space, both patient and staff, and it would more likely be a comedy than a drama.

Megan

I developed a great friendship with Megan, a mental-health worker. She was in her mid-twenties, close to my age. She was a very hard worker, full of energy, who didn't buy into all that psychotherapy talk. She believed it wasn't healthy to focus on 'issues' all day with no break. Megan provided me with an escape from the analytical eyes of the staff and doctors. She provided a brief glimpse of normalcy in an environment where abnormal was the norm. We broke many rules together, but only those that caused no harm. Every day she brought me candy, which was against the rules. Often, the same nurse I mentioned earlier in the coffeepot incident, in her Nazi-like way, would do thorough room searches for 'contraband.' Megan always took care of us. She would go in our room before Denise (the Nazi-nurse) under the pretense she was also looking for 'contraband,' but instead would remove any candy from our rooms and hide it in the washing machine on the unit. Megan never hesitated to ignore simple, harmless rules, but she worked hard at keeping all of us safe. Her words were always encouraging. She believed in me and became my biggest cheerleader. When I left on pass to attend my high school graduation ceremony, it was she who arrived to support me and reinforce my confidence in her. And after my discharge, when I was lost and struggling to find my way, it was she who filled my days with healthy activities such as tennis, shopping and eating. She saw the potential in me at a time I was certain my life would end in suicide. She was *Grace*. She broke many rules and was ultimately terminated from the hospital because of that, but Megan was the key to my survival after my discharge. She did the things with me that the doctors and nurses couldn't because of professional boundaries. She was there to fill my time with movies, music, sports and new restaurants; she showed me the good things life had to offer.

Megan brought fun to the hospital. One night, I was feeling cooped up and smothered. She took me off the unit around 9:00 p.m. We walked to the administrative building, took the keys to the hospital van and drove around town, stopping for ice cream. We brought the van back before anyone knew what we had done. When I said we broke all the rules, I meant we broke them *all*!

Discharge Plans

Within days of Hannah's removal, my planned discharge was complete. As I drove away from the hospital, I was amazed how fast it felt to ride in a car. Car trips had been few in those eight months and it felt something like a roller coaster. There were many things I needed to re-acquaint myself with. One was the very freedom I complained about losing in the beginning. I didn't trust my own actions out of the hospital. My safety net was gone. In the hospital, even if I wanted to hurt myself, I couldn't, but once out, I was really unsure if the coping skills I learned while hospitalized would work. I was completely lost. All my friends from high school had graduated and moved away to college.

Even if they were still in town, they had no idea how to approach me. The rumors in my small town were wilder than anything I could have created myself. The community in which I grew up was quite unforgiving. It was a perfect setup for another failure.

I had learned many lessons during my stay at the hospital, but one that has stayed with me through the years is compassion. I am far less likely to judge people by choices they have made or are making, because exposing me to other people with life experiences as bad or worse than mine has softened my heart. I learned that people really do the best they can with what they have. Sometimes their best isn't very good at all, but all choices are an attempt to meet a need. I hesitate to imagine where my journey would have taken me had I not been surrounded by caring, concerned people who accepted my shortcomings and helped me grow out of them. As I age, I find that basic lesson has endured and my tolerance for differences has grown because of it.

Lisa

Lisa played a huge role in my life during my stay at the hospital. Desperation is not an endearing quality, and unfortunately, that was my most obvious feature at the time. Yet, Lisa was my support during periods of desperation. She never judged me and allowed my extreme behavior to spend itself in a loving, accepting environment. Her gentle, quiet and honest approach never lessened her ability to show me how my behavior was not the most effective way to communicate my needs. I never left a conversation with Lisa feeling embarrassed, ashamed, or belittled, yet she consistently showed me a better way to make my needs known. She offered acceptance no matter how acute those needs were. She valued my thoughts and showed respect even when my behavior was time-consuming and exhausting. Lisa taught me boundaries. When I arrived at the hospital, I had none. Even though they lacked certain knowledge of the ongoing sexual abuse, everyone on the staff intuited it from the beginning. Lisa taught by example; she showed me through her interactions with me what appropriate boundaries were. It was a hard lesson to learn, but her consistency in practicing good boundaries with me finally sunk in and I draw upon that knowledge even today. I consciously include it in the development of my girls. The lessons Lisa taught me about boundaries would one day be used to sever the relationship with Father Michael, even though Lisa had no knowledge of Father Michael until years after my discharge from the hospital.

I grew to adore Lisa. Often, Lisa tipped the scale for survival and against suicide. She was the one contact during my stay at the hospital who offered me hope and security. God placed her there at exactly the right juncture to save my life. She was one of those spiritual mothers that I often speak of, another bridge that kept me from the swirling, black waters below. She showed me patience, acceptance, and empathy at a time when I felt alone, confused and misunderstood. She was subtle in her approach, but extremely effective at her job. It was as if God wired her specifically to work with adolescents lost in the maze of depression and bad choices. She had something significant and meaningful to bring to this world and her gifts and talents were not wasted. In fact, those gifts saved my life.

Chapter 6: Career by Destiny

My education and career path were chosen by the circumstances in my life during my teenage years. Suicidal thoughts dominated my thinking during this time. In fact, I never pondered or dreamed about what I would like to do in my adult years. I never expected to live past eighteen, so dreams of a career, wedding, or family of my own were never entertained. When my graduation from high school rolled around, I was still hospitalized and still focused on ending my life, yet there I stood at the major crossroad of life. I can't think of a greater decision to make than to decide what to do after high school. It affects who you will become, who your life-long friends will be, and even whom you may marry. Should I continue with further education or not? If I did choose further education, where? Would it be a four-year university? A trade school? I didn't even know what my interests were because I never allowed any to develop. I had gone through just enough therapy to believe that I might actually have a chance at success in the game called life. Imagine trying to make a life-altering decision while committed to a psychiatric treatment facility. In the hospital, I didn't have the luxury of visiting college campuses or a college guidance counselor. My high school guidance counselor, Mrs. Winn, was extremely active with me throughout all four years of high school, but we never once discussed post-graduation plans and goals. Perhaps, like me, she was just focused on keeping me alive.

The idea to become a nurse had nothing to do with altruistic thoughts. My best friend at the time wanted to become a nurse and spent a great deal of time speaking with my mother, who is an RN, about what was required for admission to nursing school. Since I had no wish-dreams and the nursing school provided books, tuition, uniforms and dormitory in exchange for post-graduation employment, I went along with the idea. My focus was on finding a place to live after release from the hospital. There were no funds for higher education for me and I fell into that bracket of kids whose parents made too much for financial aid, but not enough to pay for college tuition. This nursing school was the same one that my mother had attended and going there made sense at the time. My grandmother was an RN. My mother was an RN, and so I would become a third-generation RN. This was to be my destiny.

Chapter 7: The Most Devastating Event of My Life

Shortly after my discharge from the hospital, Father Michael attended a swimming party at my parents' home. We walked around to the front on the house and sat on the sidewalk. He began to speak in a gentle, parental voice. His tone was soft, sincere and nurturing; yet, what he said was shocking beyond belief and out of harmony with his tone. He told me how he wanted to take me back to his apartment and lie naked with me, and he went on from there. I immediately started crying because I realized that all those years, my gut feelings were right.

I said, "I was right, all those years."

"No, no, no, you were a child then," he replied. "I would never have done anything to hurt you, but you are eighteen now. Come with me."

Shocked and shaken, I rose, entered the house, and told my mother of the conversation. Until that moment, she had no idea what was going on. She adored Father Michael, and all priests for that matter. In response to my cry for help, she walked away. No words, no emotion.

The most devastating event of my life had just occurred. When I needed rescuing the most, when I was the most vulnerable, she walked away.

What did I do? Hopeless, I followed him to his apartment as he had asked and allowed him the freedom to do as he wished. For the first time, I knew for certain that he was doing wrong. I no longer needed acceptance, compassion, or to feel worthy. Instead I felt self-destructive, self-abusive and suicidal. It was truly the worst day of my life.

Father Michael had moved out of the rectory. I am unsure exactly why, but I suspect it was to avoid the ever-watchful eyes of the secretaries and other members of the church staff. Having his own apartment gave him the privacy to expand his grooming. Driving by this apartment today still causes me to become nauseous and shaky. To me, it feels as if there was an evil, sinister presence there.

When I walked through his front door, I was still hopeful that what he had described on my parents' sidewalk would not happen. My mother's response was devastating and had left me in real need of a comforting, understanding mentor. Instantly, he led the way to his bedroom. I resisted and sat down in his living room instead.

"Please, can this be different? Can we just talk?"

"Yes, yes, of course, but just come with me."

"No, I want to stay here, in the living room."

"Truly, I would never do anything to hurt you... Please trust me."

Hesitating, resisting, I followed him into his bedroom, seeing it for the first time, finding it simple but tasteful. Unlike the rectory, it had color and warmth. His bed was neatly made and in its center lay a crucifix. He lowered me sideways on the bed at the foot. He asked me if he could remove his clothes, and even as he asked, he began to undress. I began uncontrollable weeping. I had never seen a nude man before, not even in pictures, and I couldn't bear that the first man I saw was a priest. It was sacrilegious. I still saw this man as holy and reverent and to see him exposed and nude would be devastating.

At the sight of my tears, he quickly re-dressed and lay down next to me. For the next hour or so, we just talked. It was good and I relaxed and let my defenses down.

Then out of the blue, he asked me to remove my blouse, explaining that he wanted to see the beauty God had made. I declined, and thus began a dance: he asking and I refusing until I was emotionally exhausted and allowed him to remove the blouse. I eventually ended up lying on his bed dressed only in my bra and panties. I had nothing left to offer. I was empty inside and humiliated beyond expression so I turned my head away and as I did, the crucifix on his bed caught my gaze. It became my focal point. I didn't even want to blink.

As he ran his hands along my body, he kept asking me to remove my bra and panties. I kept saying 'no' without taking my gaze off of the crucifix. I wasn't crying; I wasn't even emotional; I was numb. As his hand moved toward the crucifix to sweep it to the floor, he asked if he could put his fingers inside me. I lost control. My focal point was gone. When the crucifix hit the floor I felt completely abandoned. I was lying on the bed with Satan—destined to be connected to him for the rest of my life. I left immediately. I don't remember how, but I know I did not allow him to penetrate me. On the way home, I was violently sick. I stopped at a garbage dumpster and threw the bra and panties into it. No matter how many showers I took, I could not get clean.

As a result of that encounter, engaging in sexual intimacy became difficult for me, even in the healthiest, most committed relationship of marriage. It doesn't matter how lovingly my husband may look at me—I always see Father Michael's eyes. As I look back, I wonder why I allowed him to undress me, but would not allow him to undress. I seemed to feel that I was already broken and damaged, but I still saw him as free of original sin. I was expendable, but he was precious… chosen by God to do His work. Even today as I write this, I am filled with shame and I wonder if I will have the courage to share this writing with those who would benefit from it. This has been the most difficult portion of the story to write because of my responsibility in it. The words were difficult to type and have yet to cross my lips.

The entire relationship with Father Michael struck me as incestuous. The repulsive, sickening emotions evoked when imagining a sexual relationship with a father or uncle also surfaced with a priest. Father Michael incarnated everything a parent should be. Therefore, experiencing him as a potential sexual partner produced great turmoil and confusion. From my perspective, it was not puppy love or a crush. Rather, I experienced it more the way one would feel in the presence of a childhood sports hero, an unrealistic infatuation based on status instead of character and goodness. The incestuous feelings stirred in me an urgent need to escape.

The fallout from that visit was tremendous. That week, tormented by mental tapes of that day that played relentlessly again and again, I decided to end my life. I felt insignificant and expendable. I believed I was just a trinket to be played with by Father Michael and I knew that no one even noticed. My stomached ached with turmoil that day and as the ten o'clock evening news came on, I left my room with my journal, my Bible, my teddy bear and a butcher knife. I drove to the closest car wash. With the butcher knife, I cut a hose from a vacuum cleaner, just as Hannah had taught me to do during my stay at the hospital. I drove to a nearby Catholic church and parked my car on the lot adjacent to the church, but away from the rectory and any activity. Very methodically, I stuck the hose to the end of the exhaust and ran it through my car window, just had Hannah had taught me to do.

I stuffed the crack in the window with my jacket to trap more of the toxic fumes inside the car. I took two Ativan pills, an anti-anxiety agent to help me relax and sleep. I sat in the driver's seat, turned on the engine and began to read from the Bible and write in my journal. It instantly became hot inside the car, but I did not want to turn on the air conditioner because I was afraid the fresh air would prolong my attempt. I began to sweat. The fumes irritated my throat and I started to cough. My eyes began to tear and burn to the point that it was difficult to see. Whoever said this method of carbon monoxide poisoning was a painless option for suicide obviously had never tried it. It was a miserable experience. I started to feel sleepy, and wanted to lie down. I crawled into the back seat to get more comfortable and drifted off to sleep. The only way to escape the pain was sleep.

Father John, the pastor of that church, found me several hours later.

I awoke to the piercing sound of an ambulance siren. Startled and confused, I jumped in the driver's seat to drive away, but was disoriented and seeing double. The world was spinning as I tried to remember where I was, what had happened and what I was doing. I stopped just short of a telephone pole when I realized I couldn't see straight enough to drive. Once stopped, I remembered the night before and my plan. I had failed and I grew angry. I was angry at the Emergency Medical Technicians who worked with me. I was angry at Father John who found me and disturbed my attempt. To this day, I wonder what he was doing up so late.

I had purposely waited until late in the night, to assure that everyone was asleep. I was angry at my parents for their embarrassment when they appeared in the emergency room. And, I was angry at the medical staff that cared for me at the hospital because of their insensitive and unforgiving attitude. It was if my crisis robbed them of precious time with other patients who had *real* problems. They were resentful and didn't try to hide it. They did not acknowledge that I had a life-threatening condition even though it was self-induced. No one recognized the anguish and turmoil I was feeling. No empathy for the unbearable pain that would induce a near-suicide. The reaction of the emergency room staff that night has haunted me all these years. Perhaps that is why my heart is filled with compassion for those who are depressed and suicidal.

After my discharge from the medical hospital, I returned to the same psychiatric treatment facility, which had just discharged me. This time, I was admitted to the adult unit with a bunch of forty-something people who were making the same mistakes I was. Although I hated it at the time, it was an excellent decision by my doctors. The adult unit had none of the staff I knew and loved, and the patients impressed me as weird and pathetic. I realized my life was headed in that direction and I would be there twenty years later if I did not change my behavior.

I chose not to participate in any of the therapies, thus leaving me completely bored and disengaged. My discharge came only three days later, not because I was better, but because my oldest brother's baby had died after childbirth. My mother convinced them to let me out.

The day after my discharge, I attended my infant nephew's funeral in the same church where I had attempted suicide earlier in the week. Ironically, Father John performed the service. A crowd of emotions rushed through me: sadness for my brother, embarrassment as I heard the whispers of gossip, disappointment that the grave I was standing over wasn't for me, and shock at the tiny size of an infant's casket. Hopeless, disillusioned, despondent, frustrated, angered, trapped, confused, desperate, lost and totally alone—all this summed up my existence.

One of my on-going struggles in forgiving myself revolved around the choices I made in relation to Father Michael who abused me. At first, I was unsure his actions were abusive and I dismissed them as showing affection in a fatherly way. Then, as I started to suspect something wrong, I met with him just to check out my suspicions. That made me a partner in his plan. His method of grooming kept me guessing whether his behavior was appropriate or not. If I was hesitant or tried to leave, he would smile and very calmly explain that 'this' was love and God looked favorably on sharing love and that 'this' was in no way violating his vows.

If his rationalization did not persuade me, he used guilt in the most effective way; explaining that in Ireland you are pressured to become a priest and are sent away to the seminary at age fourteen, before you are old enough to know what life is about. He would describe the loneliness of the priesthood and how, when a priest dies, there is no family at the graveside to mourn his death. It was quite pitiable, and it always worked. His manipulation was refined to the point that he never admitted that any inappropriate actions had ever happened. His 'amnesia' always left me doubting my own sanity. Even when the abuse became blatantly wrong, I could be convinced otherwise.

Once when I arrived at his door, he greeted me totally nude. In shock, I turned away, but he insisted he had just showered, hadn't had time to dress, and asked me to wait at the door until he could put clothes on. He had just moved into a new garage apartment where the bedroom was up a spiral staircase. As he showed me his new home, I went up the stairs first and he followed, and as he climbed the stairs, he again removed his clothes. I was unaware of this until we reached his bedroom. It's funny the things you remember... his entire body was completely tanned with no swimsuit lines. I kept wondering how that happened. It was better to focus on those details, than the present moment. Why didn't I just leave? I couldn't. He gave me just enough of what I was so desperate for: kindness, attention, and compassion. Those were the days when I was on the brink of suicide. His words would comfort me and he would encourage me to endure. That part of the relationship kept me in the game. He was so compassionate and understanding that I could forgive the bad part of the relationship.

Looking back with the wisdom and knowledge I have gained, I now question Father Michael's true needs. At first glance, I thought it was a basic physiological need. All human beings, after all, were designed to be sexual—even celibate priests. But something has haunted me all these years. Never once was there an erection, orgasm, or ejaculation. At the time, I didn't know these things should occur in a normal, healthy sexual encounter. Only after I had engaged in a healthy sexual relationship did I understand the physiological process. So, the way in which I justified and excused the abuse was based on my idea of the basic human need denied him by the priesthood.

When I realized that his behavior had little or nothing to do with physiology, I became alarmed and disturbed. If it wasn't a physical need, what was it? I shudder to think what it really was. The sexual abuse was mixed with religious symbols that I revered as holy and sacred. They were used to convince me that the abuse was appropriate, that God's hands were guiding the action and He was directing the scene for His own pleasure. Despite all the work in therapy, I will always keep those moments when sexual abuse and religious symbols collided in a very sick and devastating way, private in my heart. I'm afraid more work will have to take place after my death when I can have that conversation directly with God. Until that time, I struggle with God's plan and purpose for my life. As my husband and I searched for a church home, it was in the forefront of my mind. I literally had to unlearn all I was taught—which made it difficult to discern what was right and good.

I have long grieved the loss of this man as my friend and confidant. It is difficult to write this story because, when people hear of the abuse, he is automatically labeled 'bad.' People don't understand that each person is made up of different parts, some good and some not so good. It is impossible for me to categorize him as 'bad.' There were many good and kind parts to this man, which is why I remained confused and unsure of his intentions. It is also why it is so difficult to express anger toward him.

Chapter 8: Charles

I came straight from the hospital to nursing school and found that dorm life mirrored the structure of the hospital routine in many ways. Instead of group therapy, we had study groups. I loved dorm life. I had a roommate, but she never stayed in the room, so I had plenty of privacy if I so chose, but mostly I would leave my door open so the sounds of student life could permeate my room. It was a lively environment and there was always something to do or someone to talk to. I don't remember feeling lonely or sad in nursing school, perhaps because the academics kept us so focused. But, what I remember most about nursing school was falling deeply in love with one of my classmates.

Charles was nineteen years older, but I didn't notice. He was fun-loving, gentle and altogether spontaneous. He planned for nothing. To this day, I have not met anyone else with such a strong sense of work ethic. Eventually, that work ethic would play a crucial role in our separation. He loved animals more than anyone I had met before. Nursing was his second career. He had graduated from a state university with a degree in Wildlife Biology. He spent his life working on ranches throughout the region, and even while in nursing school, he lived on and managed a ranch. Despite his innate lack of planning, he pursued nursing because he realized that wildlife biology did not offer him the income or benefits to support him through retirement.

Our courtship developed slowly at first. We were always assigned to the same clinical group, so there was plenty of time to get to know each other. Eventually, I would take trips with him to the ranch. We would ride for hours in the open Jeep looking at wildlife. Once, he even chased a porcupine up a tree, and using a tree limb, gently tapped the porcupine so it would surrender a few quills. It was the first gift I received from him… unique and quite original! Life was an adventure with him. We would lie in the back of an open bed pick-up truck watching the night sky. The Milky Way was brilliant away from the city lights. When Halley's Comet became visible, we spent each evening gazing through a telescope at its beauty. We would hop on a plane and fly to Houston just to spend the day at an amusement park. We would drive to the coast just in time for the sunrise, eat breakfast and drive back. For me, it was magical, the first time I felt happy and free. On many nights we would stay up the whole night talking and arrive for clinicals the next morning at 6:30 without a wink of sleep. The ranch hosted many quiet, romantic bonfires with roasted hotdogs, marshmallows, and hot chocolate. He was generous and thoughtful. I had once mentioned that as a child I would have loved to have a birthday party at Chuck E. Cheese's. On my next birthday, he arranged a surprise birthday party for me there with all my adult family and friends.

Once graduated from nursing school, I moved to an apartment, my first opportunity to live alone. It was scary. I still had infrequent contact with Father Michael, but mostly by phone conversations. I believed that I had finally learned to identify Father Michael's traps and resist his requests. Shortly after moving to my new apartment, I received a call from him requesting a visit to my apartment. He said he had something he needed me to proofread for him. I accepted with some hesitation. Each time I met with him, I believed the encounter would be different and his intentions would not be so self-serving. On this visit, I was looking for acknowledgement of what had happened and an apology. Instead, he told me he was writing a book and wanted me to proofread a chapter for him. When I read the chapter, it was about two single men meeting on a beach and having sex in a port-a-potty. I was embarrassed and humiliated once again, and asked him to leave.

Meanwhile, Charles and I discussed marriage. We put a lot of thought into it. We were aware of the age difference and the challenges that would present. We were of different faiths. Although he grew up in the First Christian Church, he did not attend services and felt that nature was his temple. At that point I was still tied to the Catholic faith. The discussion of children revealed the central problem. I knew I did not want to leave this life without experiencing the joy of motherhood and all that children had to teach me. Ironically, Charles did not want to have children. He loved children, studied to be a pediatric nurse, and turned into "Patch Adams" when around them. I couldn't understand his thinking. He explained that the men in his family died young because of cardiac disease, and the early death of his own father had spoiled his desire for children. He did not want another person to experience the premature death of a parent as he had. With some pushing on my part, we agreed to compromise and have just one child. I later would regret the decision to force the issue. I was young and didn't understand that you can't fit a circle into a square. I just knew that he offered the safety, fun, and nurturing that had been lacking in my life.

In the strong Polish-Catholic community in which I grew up, huge church weddings were the rule. At ours, we hosted over four hundred guests. We had the dinner, the dance, the alcohol, and observed the whole joyful, extravagant tradition. Then came the honeymoon—an early indication of how much Charles loved wildlife. We spent several days at a Wildlife Preserve. We stayed in a wonderful bed and breakfast. Our days were filled with learning about their cheetah breading program and the precious, endangered black rhino. This did not match the vision and dreams I'd had of a honeymoon. Charles was oblivious to my needs and desires, and it was the first time I realized that his love of wildlife would always take precedence over me. Wildlife and the ranch became 'the other woman.'

After the wedding, I moved to the ranch. The owner added on to the small hunting cabin where Charles was living to accommodate his new wife. I could stand on the front porch and rotate 360 degrees and see nothing but wilderness. I could scream at the top of my lungs and be heard only by the scattering birds. The ranch was in such a remote area that it took me well over an hour one way to get to work. There was no television reception, so for our viewing pleasure every day, Charles played one of the many hunting videos from his vast collection. I hated them. Watching animals die a slow, painful death was not entertainment for me. Somehow, he thought that because he had an insatiable love of wildlife, I should possess that same love.

The fun and freedom I had experienced during our courtship was replaced with restrictions similar to those imposed by my parents in my early years. My opinion of love was youthful and naïve, for I believed if you gave all, even if that left you with nothing, you would still have more than enough for a happy existence. Growing up is painful. In my youthful optimism, I gave up my lifestyle, my job, my hobbies, my personal preferences, and my goals, dreams and wishes. The 'other woman'—the ranch—always took priority. There were many things to be done daily and if all the chores were done and everything was in order, Charles would initiate other projects just for fun. There was always the promise of time together when 'this' was done, but 'this' usually took all day until late in the evening, so there was no time or energy for anything except sleep. The next day started with the same promise, never fulfilled.

I sat for hours picking the weeds out of the pebble driveway. It might have been relaxing if it had been my driveway. I stood outside in the freezing rain to help gut a deer that I had no part in killing and no plans to eat. I sat in a lonely, isolated deer blind in the pre-dawn hours with frozen feet and hands because it was 'wonderful.' I felt I was dying a slow and miserable death.

The main ranch house that we helped maintain was a multi-million-dollar building. It was rustic, but with every imaginable luxury. It had a wrap-around porch with white rockers and a large limestone fireplace. The house sat upon a hill and looked down on a cascading waterfall into a spring-fed pool that spilled over into a lake. There was a large cliff to the right of the lake, and at the push of a button, a dramatic waterfall crashed into the calm waters below. I sat for hours in those rocking chairs feeling alone and lost. My soul longed for the energy of the city. When had I given away my identity? I was living someone else's life; yet I couldn't complain because I had agreed to it all... in exchange for the promise of a child. But Charles didn't meet his end of the bargain. He was waiting for me to *LOVE* the ranch before he committed to having a child.

My sexual relationship with Charles was completely unbalanced. He had a healthy sex drive, willing to engage in spontaneous sex anywhere. I was reserved, shy and completely inexperienced. My knowledge of sex was limited to what Father Michael had shown me and I couldn't rely on that because I had 'forgotten' Father Michael and my earlier struggles. I stuffed those memories so deep inside me that I could look someone in the eye and deny ever even having been Catholic. With

Charles, I learned that physical satisfaction might be attainable and could see that sexual intimacy had something significant to offer. Sadly, however, I never accepted what it had to offer. My sexual relationship with Charles mirrored the same dance I'd had with Father Michael. He asked, I declined, eventually giving in so I could be left alone. Most of the time, I went through the motions, with no emotion except disgust and regret.

There is much I can say that went wrong with my marriage to Charles. I wasn't equipped to handle the responsibility of marriage and the intimacy it entails. The sexual demons inhabiting my soul manifested themselves in ways I couldn't describe. In my time with Charles, I was unfair to him in many ways. I could not handle the intensity of emotions brought on by intimacy. I struggled to explain to him things I could not consciously know and even at that point, several years out of the hospital, I found myself focused on self-abuse and suicide. Intimacy brought flashbacks that frightened me. One of Charles' great gifts was to sit up with me each night as these terrifying images pushed their way to the surface. He protected me at times when I was a danger to myself, and it is that protection that endeared me to him for all those years. My unprocessed, unacknowledged trauma from Father Michael challenged Charles, and I can only imagine the level of frustration and confusion he must have felt.

Despite the drama of our marriage, Charles and I had enough respect and admiration for each other that when the time came to separate, we did so with dignity and grace. I am exceedingly proud of how we each handled our divorce. We were able to end the marriage without ending the friendship. We calmly talked out the settlement. We chose not to employ a lawyer, since there was nothing to dispute. We drove together to the court house on the day of our divorce and celebrated our friendship with a meal at a local café afterward. Early on, we had agreed never to let our marriage continue so long that we became enemies. We each honored that and a genuine friendship has lasted because of our commitment. I couldn't imagine hating the person I once loved beyond measure. What a different world we would have if everyone could part in such a way!

This is what my marriage to Charles taught me: **NEVER** sell yourself short. When I learned that my desires, needs, and values were just as important as his, I left and never looked back. I came out of that marriage strong, mature and ready to live life my way. I moved back to the city, started competitively roller-skating again, bought a house, lost fifty pounds, and developed great friendships. I thrived back in the city. I enjoyed my house and decorated it with pinks, blues and lace. I didn't want anything masculine there… especially not deer heads hanging on the walls. This was my space, my haven, my retreat and I surrounded myself with the things that brought me comfort and peace. The period after my divorce was the first time in my life when I focused on what made me happy, yielding to no one. I learned more about myself during that time. It proved to be a remarkable gift that provided the strength I needed to report the abuse to the Catholic Church. Also, the divorce enabled me to quiet the demons of sexual abuse stirring in me because I was no longer confronted with sexual reminders. The dormancy of the demons allowed me to 'forget' any and all abuse. I didn't use the strength I had gained.

My first marriage taught me what was sexually appropriate and what was not. Even while I was married, Father Michael continued to seek a relationship with me. He contacted my mother in order to locate me, and, being in denial of the abuse, she gave him my work number. He started to call me at work. Once again, he requested a meeting, and once again, I accepted… only this time I would not meet him in private, so we met at a local Mexican restaurant. He had aged tremendously. As he sat drinking his scotch and water, he attempted an apology, though he never clearly stated what he was sorry for. That was supposed to be understood, but his small offering was not what I expected or needed. I wanted him to acknowledge what had happened, that I didn't make it up, and that he had groomed me all those years for his personal satisfaction. I left disillusioned. When he continued to call, I asked him never to contact my family or me again. He honored my request.

Chapter 9: *"The Church of Hospice"*

Somewhere along this journey, I discovered hospice. After graduation from nursing school, I worked on a telemetry unit for a year or so before internalizing the reality of my own mortality. I knew there had to be a better way to die than in a cold hospital room on a hard, plastic mattress, dressed in a thin gown that robbed the last hint of dignity. I saw countless people die slow, painful and invasive deaths because no one had taken the time to tell them about other options.

I participated in many 'codes,' where someone's heart stopped beating. While doing chest compressions to re-start a worn-out and reluctant heart, I would wonder what the spirit was doing and how sad it must be to have your chest pounded with the full weight of another adult, to hear and feel your ribs cracking beneath their hands. The trauma of seeing an endo-tracheal tube crammed downed a patient's throat nauseated me, but the worst was to watch a patient's heart give out on the telemetry monitor. The blip of a heartbeat on the screen slowly fades away to an eerie flat line. I often wondered at what point the spirit left the body.

It was in the care of actively dying patients and their post-mortem care where I found my true gifts and abilities. Actively dying is a term used in hospice to describe a patient in the last hours of life. I blossomed in these moments and for the first time felt as if my life had meaning and purpose. I had a hospice heart and moved away from curative medicine into a movement that took all aspects of a person into account: physical, emotional, spiritual, and financial. Holistic therapies were welcomed and encouraged, but more importantly, patients were allowed to live out their days in comfort and in the environment of their choosing. Hospice was the service farthest from the medical model I could find without sacrificing the benefits of the very model I was trying to escape.

Working with hospice patients came very easy to me. I took time to get to know each of them. On slow days, I would spend time looking through their family albums, listening to their stories that had been told a thousand times, but that I was hearing for the first time. As I looked at the black and white photos yellowed with age, I saw that the people in those snapshots were young, with the zest for life spilling from their eyes. They weren't that different from me and it was in these moments that I realized that I, too, would grow old and in my old age would look back on the memories I was making today. This lesson held more value than any I learned in therapy. My outlook on life started to change and my motto became, "the secret to life is to enjoy the passage of time."

Shortly after my divorce, I was visiting with a patient who explained that she was a member of the All-American Women's Baseball League during World War II. Her eyes lit up as she shared stories of her glory days. She asked me if I was involved in any sports. I told her that I competed as a child in artistic roller-skating, but had to quit because of circumstances out of my control. I shared the regret in my heart, and that I had not been ready to give up the sport.

Nationals 1999: Syracuse, New York.

She looked at me with a matter-of-fact expression and asked, "Well, why aren't you skating now? You are young and healthy; go; do; live!"

Her words were life-changing for me. She was right; I had wasted much of my life in the darkness of depression. The very next day, I drove an hour and a half to the roller rink to take my first skating lesson. When I laced up my skates, I had the same rush of excitement I felt as a child. I skated every day, several hours a day, competed in Nationals and met my future husband. As a result of a single conversation with that precious hospice patient, my life changed dramatically. I pursued my dream of skating, married my soul mate and created two beautiful daughters. Everyone has a purpose, even when it appears as if their life is already over. This is the lesson that sweet lady taught me. She never knew the impact of her words because she died a few days after that conversation. Perhaps one of her purposes in this life was to give me back my own.

When people asked me, "What religion are you?" I wouldn't say that I am Catholic or Christian. I would say, "I belong to the church of hospice." It always left people intrigued and I explained that my spiritual needs were being met through my ministry in hospice. The near death awareness that my patients experienced was the nourishment for my soul. For instance, I took care of a remarkable woman who was Catholic and believed very much in angels. She was the matriarch of her family, the rock and the pillar. She had an amazing, gracious strength that instantly set her apart and made her unique among my other patients.

She was diagnosed with the cruel disease of Ovarian Cancer. As the tumor grew, she developed a bowel obstruction that eventually sealed off her colon and prohibited any further passage of stool. She became perpetually nauseated, stopped eating and her abdomen grew to look as if she was in the third trimester of pregnancy. The prognosis was grim, and as I sat with her that day, I had to explain that in the days preceding her death, she would continue to vomit her own stool. I assured her that I would aggressively work at keeping her comfortable—even using terminal sedation if necessary. The news was ominous and hopeless, but she looked at me with great strength and smiled.

All she said was, "I believe in angels."

I smiled back with an understanding of her faith and said, "Well, when you see your angels, will you let me know?"

Three weeks passed; she continued to vomit despite giving her medication to halt all function of the gastrointestinal tract. I went to visit her; it was a Friday and I would not be on-call that night. I knew she would die that night so I stopped by to check on her and to say my goodbyes. By this time, her body had wasted away to about sixty pounds. She looked like a concentration camp victim. She was still alert, although frail and tired. Her words were now a barely audible whisper, clear, but slow in coming.

As I sat next to her bed brushing her hair, she looked up at me, and in the tiniest whisper said, "I haven't seen my angels yet."

I was heart-broken and worried that I had erred when I asked her to let me know when she saw her angels. I was young in my hospice experience and didn't know what to say, so I said nothing. I left her home feeling that I had failed as her nurse because I could not relieve her unforgiving nausea and relentless pain and that I had falsely given her hope where there was none.

The following morning I was on-call. My pager went off about 9:00 in the morning and it was Elsa's daughter. She tearfully but quietly explained that her mom had died in the night but the last few hours were peaceful and symptom free. Before she died, all the grimaces and frowning had relaxed and a soft, peaceful smile replaced her look of agony. Her daughter repeated her final words for me, and I was forever touched. Elsa's last words were, "Tell Crystal I saw my angels and how pretty and white their wings were. Tell her they made me snow." I was relieved to know her pain was gone and comforted to know there was a loving God waiting for her on the other side. She had seen her angels and for this family, my work was done.

Understanding the power of Elsa's story, I purchased a sterling silver angel charm to place on my bracelet. Each time someone asks me the story behind the charm, I proudly and warmly tell the story of Elsa and her angels to honor her and to remember her undying faith. So, when people would ask me, "What religion are you?" I would respond, "The church of hospice" and then share this story as well as many others just like this one.

Working with hospice patients brought me closer to God and daily challenged my beliefs. I worked with people from all walks of life, including different religious backgrounds. I was able to listen and learn from their perspectives and grew to believe that religious views don't matter: God is a gentle being. Many times in the early hours of the morning, while I sat with a dying patient, I could physically feel His presence. I sat at the bedside and watched as people had ongoing conversations with God. I saw the child-like smile smooth their otherwise pain-ridden face and knew something greater was at work there.

The moment a person takes the last breath is the holiest I have ever witnessed. It is precious, reverent. I am acutely aware that the instant of death is unique for each human being. It is private, humbling, and it leaves everyone involved vulnerable and exposed. As a person dies, one can physically see the moment the spirit leaves the body and then the mechanics of a dying creature begin, reminding me of a child's wind up toy that slowly winds down. The stillness in the last moment is unparalleled. If one can look past the ugliness of a frail, emaciated, broken body, the actual death is peaceful and beautiful. The weeks and months preceding the death are the painful part.

Most deaths happen in the dark early morning hours between 3:00 and 4:00, perhaps because all is quiet. The business of the day doesn't get in the way of the dying process. I would awake suddenly to the sharp sound of the pager alarm. After scrambling for the phone, I would hear a family member describe the symptoms of someone actively dying. After dressing, still half asleep, I would drive to the patient's home. There would always be family members anxiously waiting for me at the door as if I were going to give them different news than what they were expecting. I would greet the family and make my way to the room where the dying person lay. As I entered the room, several family members, usually women, would look up at me with that same hope in their eyes. I could see that they had been there for hours, performing a death vigil, afraid to leave for a moment, in case the person would take that last breath while they stepped out. I acknowledged their anguish and each time was amazed at what the human spirit can endure in the face of great emotional stress.

I was beginning to understand that each of us has pain and regret in our lives. We all choose different ways of dealing with it. As I gently assessed the patients, the immediate family would remain. I would hear painful stories of regret, joyous stories of great times and hysterical anecdotes about their life. I would not leave a patient who was actively dying, offering to stay and provide physical and emotional support to the exhausted family. In those pre-dawn hours, we perused family photo albums. I listened to stories of how the person met their spouse along with the courtship and marriage. I would hear horrifying stories of men who endured World War II and how they persevered despite great tragedy around them. Each of these patients was helping me grow, evolve, and blossom into the woman I am today. Each of their stories remains with me; their families are with me, helping me along my journey. Years have passed since my work with those patients and families, but collectively, they taught me patience, compassion, and tenderness.

I know there are theories that suggest that near-death awareness is from chemical and hormonal imbalances caused by dehydration, malnutrition and tumor invasion; and perhaps, there is validity to those theories, but I have sat at the bedside of hundreds of patients and watched as their breath slowly ebbed away. I have seen them reaching for a light in the room that I could not see. I have heard them re-uniting with deceased family members and seen the look of a child on Christmas day on their faces as they witness sights unseen by me. Patients who were still conscious could describe in detail what they were seeing and hearing. These experiences give me great hope in things to come and allow me to continue to be surrounded by death in the work I choose to do. Each time I witness the peace that comes over a person close to death, I am spiritually fed. My work in hospice kept me close to God during a time when religion caused more pain than hope.

To explain better how God revealed himself to me during my work in hospice, let me share another story of a patient's experience that healed my soul. Helen was a vibrant red-head who was extremely thin because of cancer's attack her body. She was diagnosed with pancreatic cancer, a fast-moving disease with a quick but painful death. One day, when I drove up to the house, the daughter came running out. She met me at my car before I could even turn the engine off. She was out of breath and excited.

I stepped out of the car, alarmed, and she panted, "You have to go deal with Mom; I can't handle her. She's hallucinating."

I entered the room where Helen, looking long, thin and gaunt, lay on the bed. Our eyes met and a radiant, joyful smile lit her face, with no evidence of discomfort in her expression or gestures. She was giggling and waving toward the back wall of the room.

I smiled and said, "Hey, what's up?"

She said, "Don't you see them all standing there?"

"No," I replied, "I don't, but tell me about them."

She explained that against the wall stood several small children, waving to her and motioning her to "come on." I acknowledged her experience and then excused myself. I walked into the living room and sat down with the daughter. I explained that, perhaps, her mother was not hallucinating, but instead was transitioning.

Transitioning is a term often used in end-of-life care when the dying person starts to interact with beings unseen. They may have conversations with deceased family members, God, Jesus, their pets, or other people unknown to them. They tend to have periods of withdrawal from caregivers and material things once important to them. Their focus is on the unseen, until they return to be emotionally, physically, and spiritually present with the caregivers and family once more. This transitioning period can often be distressing to family members who have tirelessly cared for their loved one without restraint. Explaining to a caregiver this stepping, fluctuating between a physical plane and an intangible, spiritual plane eases their hurt and anxiety about their loved one's odd behavior.

After my well-considered explanation, I encouraged the daughter to drag a chair up to her mother's bedside. I urged her to ask her mother about the visions she was seeing, the conversations she was hearing and the feelings she was experiencing. Helen was on the fence between this world and the world she would enter when her physical body would give out. Her daughter had the opportunity to glimpse the world her mother would soon enter. It provided great comfort to Helen's daughter to view her 'hallucinations' in a positive and enlightening way. I ended my visit, but when I returned each week, those children unseen by myself and the daughter stood closer and closer to Helen's bed.

One summer day, as I entered Helen's room, she smiled and said, "They're at the foot of my bed now."

I nodded. "Well, then when you're ready, you take their hands and go."

To my surprise, she replied, "Okay, but I want to wait forty-five more minutes."

I thought this strange, but then I asked her if she wanted me in the room or out. I wanted to know if she wanted to go alone.

She peacefully replied, "I think I want to go alone."

I left to get her daughter, and after explaining my conversation with Helen, offered the daughter time with her mother to say good-bye. She visited with her mother for a while as I waited in the living room. Once done, she left the room, made a pot of coffee and then joined me on the sofa to reminisce about her mother's life. After about one hour, I peaked into Helen's room. Her spirit was gone. There was no breath, no heartbeat. Helen had died exactly as she had chosen. I never understood what the forty-five minutes were for, but it was the first time I realized that everyone *has* to die alone.

Regardless of the number of people holding a death vigil at the bedside, a loved one cannot accompany a dying person through death. They can be present up to the moment of death, but once the last breath is taken, the dying person must go alone. In working with families who are caring for a dying loved one, I often encourage them to take breaks from the bedside of an actively dying person. Dying is the most private thing you can do. It is more private that using the restroom; it is more private than having sex or giving birth. Some people need the privacy to let go. If a person does not need that privacy, I have also witnessed a dying patient hang on until whoever needs to be in the room returns. Often family members become upset if the person died in their absence and I have always viewed this as a final gift for those family members. I have discovered that more times than not, things happen exactly as they should even if it doesn't seem so at the time.

Helen's frequent visitors from beyond confirmed my belief that there is something significant and profound waiting for us at the end of this physical life. I struggled with guilt and shame from abuse, but Helen's little children gave me hope. I often think of the scene in the movie *Ghost*, where Patrick Swayze's character sees small visions full of light lined up waiting for him to let go. They were supportive and peaceful and offered unconditional love. I understood that it was God's Grace speaking to me in a way I could relate to. Helen didn't know how much her visions strengthened me in a time of pain and darkness. Those were the defining moments in my life when I chose life over suicide. My work in hospice continued to bless me in ways beyond my understanding.

Chapter 10: "Put One Foot in Front of the Other, Keep Going"

After recovering from my divorce from Charles, I settled in the city where I began working for a new hospice company. The first week of my employment, I had to spend the day with Jeremy, the chaplain, seeing patients as part of my orientation. Jeremy grew up in Ireland and was a former Catholic priest. He was slender, average height. He had a receding hairline with fiery red hair. His freckles matched his hair color. His eyes were as blue as the waters of the Caribbean and were framed with long, full eyelashes. His accent and word choices were difficult to understand, but uncomfortably familiar. Father Michael, too, was Irish and had a strong accent. Jeremy's Irish accent sent me over the edge and, while riding in his car, I had a complete, unexpected meltdown. A flood of memories rushed to the surface all at once and I was not prepared for my emotional collapse. I shared my story with him, knowing I had to deal with this issue now or quit my job and ignore the God-whisper and opportunity placed before me.

Jeremy helped me get in contact with the appropriate people in the Catholic Church to report the abuse. This was the beginning of a long and painful odyssey. The very next day I received a phone call at work from Sister Evelyn, stating that she had received my name and would like to set up an appointment to hear my story. She explained that there would be a priest in the room as well. I asked her the name of the other priest, and when I heard his name, I gasped and hung up the phone, telling her I had made a mistake. It was Father John. She immediately called me back, concerned that the priest I would meet with was the one I was about to accuse. He was not, but he was the same priest who had found me in my car some seven years before. I'd had no contact with this man in those seven years and hadn't even thought about him. I was embarrassed, ashamed and humiliated once more and it made the decision to meet with them even harder. I realized that the memories and emotions reawakened in me were God's gentle…or not so gentle nudge to encourage me forward. I honored that feeling and am grateful today that I did so.

The night before I met with them, I was a wreck. I knew they were going to want details. I was trying to come up with the words to explain what had happened without having to really explain. Thinking of the words was hard enough; I didn't think I could bear to hear the words come out of my mouth. The details had NEVER crossed my lips before. How would I find the courage to express them now?

But I had kept journals all those years. And, although I did not actually write down what was occurring, I did write down my personal struggle with it. The writings clearly related my internal battle, and there were enough inferences to make the situation clearly understood. As I sat in my bed that night reading over my words, I was struck by two things… how long ago it had been and how I had forgotten some things until I re-read them. Second, my words were very child-like and naïve.

It was easy to understand that my vocabulary and general knowledge of sex was limited to the information that Father Michael had fed me. I highlighted and dog-eared the pages I found to be helpful in explaining the circumstances.

I did not sleep that night. While I dressed, ate, and drove to the meeting, a knot clogged my throat and my stomach felt as if I were upside down on a rollercoaster. My hands were shaking, my chest beet-red, ears hot and heart racing. All the anxiety I had ever felt with Father Michael came to a head that day. Luckily, one thing I learned while hospitalized is that I have courage within me, even when I don't feel it. I knew I could call on it when I needed it. As I pulled into the parking lot and approached the doors to their office, I told myself, "Put one foot in front of the other, and keep going."

Nausea swept over me as I entered the doors. The nun came out immediately to greet me. I was grateful for that because if I had to wait, I might have talked myself out of it. My mantra of "put one foot in front of the other" failed me as I approached the office to meet with the priest who had found me in the carbon monoxide-filled car all those years before. I stopped dead and my feet would not move despite my mental commands. I now know what it means to be scared stiff.

After a few moments, I stepped inside and the door closed. It felt like a gas chamber. I stood just inside the office, not sure what to do next. They offered me a seat, which my collapsing knees gladly accepted. So, there we were, all three of us, just staring at each other. How does one begin a conversation like that? To be honest, I really don't know; I have no memory of the first few minutes.

Eventually the conversation began. I was very grateful to have brought the journals with me and I believe they found them helpful as well. The writings helped to place the abuse within a time-frame. Both Father John and Sister Evelyn were very gracious, even tearful, as my story unfolded. At the conclusion, they asked me what I was seeking. My answer was clear. I wanted therapy for me, therapy for him, and for him to be assigned to one place so he could not shift location without accountability. They honored this request.

At the conclusion of our meeting, they assured me that my requests would be fulfilled. Their most immediate job was to locate this priest and confront him with the allegations I had made. Once confronted, he denied my allegations, but was reminded that my journals were available. I was told he recanted his denial, but I was not informed of anything beyond that. For a brief time after I reported the abuse, he remained in the same city where I was living. I was in a meeting one day at work with Jeremy, the same chaplain with whom I initially shared my story, and he got up to answer a page. He was also a Licensed Professional Counselor and had a part-time practice in the evenings. The phone call was from Father Michael, who was looking for a counselor to fulfill the therapy requirements placed on him by the church. Luckily, Jeremy had enough professional common sense to not accept the case and refer him elsewhere.

When I became aware of this phone call, I became enraged and immediately went to the chancery office unannounced to discuss it. My expectation had been that there would be no contact! Although I'm sure it was an innocent mistake, why had the church not researched my case a little better? It was quite unsettling. After that, Father Michael was sent back to Ireland to pursue his therapy. I was informed that he had been 'relieved of his duties.'

A week after the initial report to the Catholic Church, I received a phone call from the Vicar General stating that the Provincial from Ireland was in town and wanted to meet with me. He explained that he was only here for a short while and that it was imperative that he meet with me that day. He requested to come to my home at once. In an attempt to be accommodating, I agreed. I was changing a flat tire, hot and filthy, but within twenty minutes of that phone call, they were knocking on my front door. Had I had a few months more therapy, I would have known how inappropriate their request was.

I was quite nervous during this meeting, unsure of their agenda. I found myself making tea for them as if it were a social call. I was in unknown territory and had no idea what was appropriate. The situation did not allow me to pick up the phone and call my mother for advice. I was flying solo, and felt that I didn't have a friend in the world. As they entered my home, I offered them a seat on the sofa. So, there I was again, staring at two representatives from the Catholic Church in an unbelievably awkward moment, but this time it was in my space… a space they were not invited into, but had entered by demand. They expected me to begin the conversation, but I was unsure what they needed.

I finally said, "I don't understand your purpose today because I have already shared my story."

At that moment I realized their purpose was to evaluate me. They wanted to know if I was believable and genuine. The Provincial was quiet and respectful during this time. He seemed embarrassed and deeply saddened at the situation. I briefly recapped my story for them.

To my surprise, the Vicar General said, "Well, you know, when you are a teenager hormones start flowing…."

He left the sentence for me to complete with the insinuation that I was the seducer. I could not believe my ears. Humiliation rushed through my veins and I shut down. It was beyond evident that their first concern was to avoid a lawsuit and a public scandal. To this day, I have never pursued civil or criminal litigation; nor have I asked for monetary compensation. The visit ended with the Vicar General standing up and requesting a final prayer with the three of us holding hands. I thought,

Are you kidding me? I found no comfort in such a prayer, and the last thing I felt comfortable doing was holding a priest's hand, but despite my thoughts, I followed their commands because of their status.

As the Vicar started the prayer *for* Father Michael, I literally swallowed the vomit rising in my throat and began my own silent prayer to survive the moment. I found the whole interview as well as the prayer to be completely insensitive, even hostile, to me. This visit was the point at which the Catholic Church as an institution fell off its pedestal. I became disillusioned with organized religion of any kind and vowed never to worship in a church again. My spiritual life was devastated. The faith I had leaned on, the only one I had ever known, had not only failed me in that single moment, it had turned against me. I will still argue that the damage done in that conversation was far greater than any endured during the sexual abuse. For the next several years, my anger was focused directly at the Catholic Church and anyone who represented it or chose it as a faith.

Within a few weeks of reporting the abuse to the church, I took a trip to Niagara Falls. I brought with me a gift I had received from Father Michael. It was an ivory colored, porcelain candy dish, oval in shape with the Irish friendship ring delicately painted in the center. It was a beautiful dish, dainty and fragile. He had brought it back from Ireland on one of his many trips back home. I truly loved this gift as it suited my personal taste; I loved it so much, in fact, that when my toddler niece dropped it on the floor and shattered it, I painstakingly glued each piece back together. Perhaps that was another of those divine whispers felt in the heart that I chose to ignore. Was God trying to show me how broken that relationship was; and, if so, did I miss the message... again?

I had brought the gift with me to Niagara Falls to drop it over as a symbolic gesture acknowledging the brokenness and end of that relationship. As I stood over the falls, I closed my eyes and tried for a moment to make time stop. I allowed myself to feel the regret and sadness in my heart. The roar of the falls was deafening, but in my soul all was quiet, although not a peaceful quiet. It was a sad, lonely quiet that had often before led my mind to drift to thoughts of suicide. As I stood there dampened by the ever-present mist, I imagined myself holding onto the gift as I released myself from the protective fence around the overlook. I pictured myself falling to the churning waters below. In my mind, I felt the shock of the impact with the icy waters. Once below the surface, I experienced the muffled quietness of swimming underwater. As a child, I often thought that death must be similar to that feeling, and to me it was familiar and comforting.

When I opened my eyes, I had not jumped into the waters and felt a pang of sadness when I turned away from the thought. I had not yet begun my therapy and the sadness I felt was only a small sample of the grief and pain I would experience in the months ahead. Therapy was so hard that had I known just how hard and how much pain I would undergo, perhaps I would have jumped that day to avoid it all! Nothing held me to this world. I had recently met my husband, but at that point he was only a friend and companion on weekends. I had no children; I lived on my own and really couldn't visualize anything of *significance* in my future—except for a God-whisper that I did hear and heed. It was God gently whispering to my heart: "*hold on, for I have plans for you.*" I didn't know what they were or when those plans would be revealed, but I trusted that they were worth waiting for and worth enduring any pain to come.

Holding the gift with both hands, I looked up to the heavens, prayed for forgiveness and with a gasp, released the gift. The dainty, delicate, treasured gift fell silently and effortlessly to the waters below. There was no sound when it landed, since the roar drowned out the sound of impact. It shattered into fragments and was instantly gone. At the time, I naively thought that the symbolic release of the gift would bring me closure and healing. Oh, if it had only been that easy!

The idea that I might not have been the only girl Father Michael abused slipped into my head when the national scandal hit the media. I realized there were many people with similar stories. Every night I would watch the evening news; fearful that Father Michael's name or my name would surface. They never did, but to this day, I am fearful of public exposure. I don't know if I would feel better that I wasn't the only one or worse because I was. I have searched his name, religious order, etc., over the internet. I have looked at the survivors' network as well as other websites, which lists priests convicted or sued because of sexual abuse. He is not on any of the lists, perhaps because he was not a diocesan priest and not from the United States.

Chapter 11: Jacob

Jacob grew up roller skating and now was giving back to the sport by judging the very events I was competing in. The owner of the rink and my coach introduced us at an Easter competition in San Antonio. Jacob was the judge; I was the skater. Jacob was living in Phoenix at the time while stationed at Luke Air Force Base where he practiced general dentistry. He had been accepted into the Oral and Maxillofacial Surgery Residency program at Wilford Hall Medical Center at Lackland Air Force Base in San Antonio and would be moving there in a couple of months.

During the skating competition, I gave him my telephone number and offered him my help in getting settled once he arrived in San Antonio to start his residency. I didn't really expect him to accept my offer of help, but a few months later, when I arrived home from work and checked my voice mail, I heard his gentle voice, saying he had made it safely to San Antonio and would love to get together for dinner. I called him back the same day and we arranged that dinner.

Our time together was like a blind date because I couldn't remember what he looked like, had only spoken to him briefly at the skating meet, and really didn't know much about him, other than that skating was a part of his life. The doorbell rang exactly at the time we had set for him to pick me up. I smiled as I climbed into his car, a Honda. I drove a Honda as well, and thought, *ah! Another thing in common.* He took me to a wonderful, quiet restaurant. I spent most of the evening listening to him talk about skating and his excitement at starting the residency. I felt shy and unsure of myself. I wasn't accustomed to dating, and my entire experience of normal interaction with a man had been with my ex-husband, Charles. I struggled to contribute to the conversation because I couldn't think of anything interesting to say that didn't include Charles. It was safer to keep asking Jacob questions about his life.

As our date came to an end, we pulled up to the entrance of my neighborhood. I lived in a gated community and had only recently purchased a home there. The remote control to open the gate was in my car and I did not know the code to open the gate manually. We sat at the entrance of the neighborhood for about thirty minutes, laughing that we couldn't get in. I was embarrassed, but found it amusing. We were hoping another car would come in or out and would open the gate for us, but that never happened. So, I crawled through the gate and walked myself home. Being the perfect gentleman, Jacob offered to escort me, but I was comfortable and somewhat relieved to walk myself home, since it did away with anxiety about the end of date kiss... or not. I smiled the whole way home, knowing what a great story it would make.

Our courtship continued. It was a hectic time. I was the clinical manager for the hospice where I was working. It was a demanding job that often left me physically and emotionally drained. Jacob struggled through the first year of residency with very little sleep and erratic

Visiting an art museum just after our engagement, 2001.

eating patterns. Despite the chaos, both of us carved out Friday and Saturday evenings for each other. That time was sacred. Many evenings, we would both be on-call and have to take separate cars to our date location, and there were many instances where our time was interrupted by the annoying sound of a pager. It was either me being pulled away to respond to a death call or Jacob answering a call about a trauma victim. I am amazed that we were ever able to fall in love. I once read an article in *Newsweek* entitled, "Fitting Your Marriage in Between the Beeps." That typified our courtship. Jacob was terribly sleep deprived, often going thirty-six hours or more without sleep, but he never cancelled a date. Too many times to count, he fell asleep during our time together… in a dark movie theatre, at a restaurant, even on the sofa in the home of my dear friend Jeremy, the hospice chaplain, and his wife, Jamie, as we were visiting over coffee and dessert. On one of our dates, we returned to Jacob's home. It was the first time I had visited his place and he was anxious for me to see it. However, when we arrived, he took a few steps inside, collapsed on the floor and was instantly asleep. Awkward doesn't describe what I felt. It was early in our dating and I still wasn't completely comfortable with him. I didn't know whether to wake him up and leave, just leave and let him continue to sleep, or wait until he woke up. I chose to wake him up to announce my departure and wish him sweet dreams. Despite all of that, we persevered, and a beautiful, simple, uncomplicated love developed because of it. I was patient with his grueling schedule and sleep deprivation and he was respectful and understanding of the demons in my closet that I had not yet introduced to him. I came to understand that this man was the closest definition of Grace that I could find and I was drawn to him like a magnet to metal.

Chapter 12: Dr. Macey

The one constant throughout this whole experience was my psychologist, Dr. Macey. As I matured, I found this woman filled with warmth and grace; although in the early years I did not experience her that way. In fact, I perceived her as cold, robotic and judgmental. I'm not sure how or when my perception of her changed, possibly through my own growth or maybe even a little of her own. I think it must have been a little of both. In the early years of therapy, I was needy, attention-seeking and very unpredictable. I can see how this woman had to maintain strict boundaries. I must have been exhausting to be around in those days.

After my discharge from the hospital, a couple of years passed without her services. When the moment came to choose a therapist to help me process the sexual abuse, I knew, despite my earlier feelings, that she was the one person who could help me the most. There was so much I didn't have to explain, so much history she had lived through with me. She knew me better than I knew myself.

This time around, I was ready to work and I understood what it meant to work in therapy. It was in these days that my perception of her changed. For the first time, I saw her as a real person with a real life. I realized she was just like me and everyone else, just working to figure it all out. It became clear that although I didn't know her struggles, I did know she was on a journey that included the same obstacles we all face. This was the connection that allowed me to share, cry, remember, and heal. I felt her patience as weeks went by, when I found myself stuck. Therapy moves ever so slowly and I think it is in such times that many people give up because they don't see immediate results. She knew exactly when to ask gently nudging questions to get me jump-started and back on track. She knew when I was feeling strong enough to hear and process the painful questions and answer them honestly. She also knew the days when I was frail, and she would adjust her style to accommodate my fragility. In these moments, I felt her compassion flow out of her like a fountain.

As I look back on my time with her, I realize that she was my companion through all the major events of my life. And although she was not physically present, through my stories she shared in my high school graduation, prom, engagement, wedding and the birth of my first daughter. More importantly, she accompanied me on my journey through an eight-month hospitalization, the hopeless moments on the brink of suicide, the report of sexual abuse to the Catholic Church, and ultimately the recovery from all of that. I will always be grateful for her encouragement and clarity. It makes my heart smile that she knows how all our hard work has paid off and that happiness and peace are my reward. Mitch Album's book speaks of *The Five People You Meet in Heaven*. For me, she would be one of those five people who have had the greatest impact on my life.

Chapter 13: Intoxicating Love

During a year and a half of dating, Jacob and I had talked frequently about marriage. By that time, we were both committed and certain that our journeys would merge in the near future. It was Christmastime in San Antonio. The river walk along the San Antonio River downtown takes your breath away at Christmas. The Cypress-lined banks of the river are aglow with hundreds of multi-colored lights, each twinkling with its own beauty. It is a magical, romantic place. On the street level, you can hear the sounds of horse-drawn carriages making their way through the narrow streets. I decided that instead of our typical date, a dinner and a movie, a carriage ride under the lights might be a nice change.

I arranged everything. This would be my treat for Jacob. I made reservations for a meal at Paesano's Italian Restaurant on the River Walk, followed by a ride in our own reserved white horse-drawn carriage. It was cold outside when we stepped out of the car. I had left my coat at the house and asked Jaccob if I could wear his. To my surprise, he said "no," but gathered my cold body and snuggled me into his as we walked to the restaurant. We had a delicious meal, but it was the dessert that we enjoyed the most. Tres Leches is a special cake drenched in cream and milk. It is amazingly moist without being soggy and has a delectable, rich flavor that is not overpowering. Eating this shared piece of cake became a sweet, memorable moment still precious to both of us years later. We were in love, the kind of mesmerizing, intoxicating love that leaves one giddy and unaware of any evil in the world. It was a great moment to share, and we lingered there enjoying the twinkling lights, Christmas music and each other's company.

When we had finished our meal, we walked up to street level. As we topped the staircase, we found ourselves in full view of Alamo Plaza. The Alamo was glowingly floodlighted, with the night sky as the dark backdrop. A huge Christmas tree filled the plaza where carolers were singing songs. We made our way to the carriage that was waiting for us by the perimeter wall of the Alamo. A weathered, kindly woman greeted us. We climbed into the carriage, covered up with a heavy, red and black flannel blanket and were on our way to see the Christmas sights to the sound of "clippity-clop, clippity-clop". For forty-five minutes, we snuggled and enjoyed the lights and each other. We would let our eyes glaze over so the colored lights would blur together. I often did this as a child during Christmas and it gave me a nostalgic feeling, warm and peaceful.

As we approached the back wall of the Alamo, Jacob realized that the time had passed quicker than he realized; our ride was almost over. He reached into his pocket and pulled a small jewelry box out and offered it to me. The look on his face was tender, genuine and completely filled with grace and love. He didn't say a word.

Without thinking, I blurted out, "Oh, I hope those aren't earrings!"

But, I then retracted a little, realizing that they might well be earrings he was giving as an early Christmas gift. When I looked up from the box, still wordless, his face reassured me that the box didn't hold earrings. I smiled.

All he said was "Well…"

I responded, "Well, I want the question."

With a look of great love and devotion, he asked, "Will you marry me?"

With a big "yes," a hug and a kiss, the carriage ride ended. The woman who was driving had been talking to us all along about the history of Alamo and both of us had been completely oblivious to her educational monologue. She was unaware of what had just happened.

We stepped out of the carriage and made our way back to the front of Alamo Plaza. Sitting next to the massive Christmas tree, I looked down at the ring now on my left hand for the first time. It was beautiful: platinum, with three princess-cut diamonds. In this moment, I felt God's presence reminding me that He had given me the strength, all those years, to hold on for this moment. The atmosphere, the environment, the temperature, and the company could not have been more perfect. In a single moment, I felt as if all my prayers from years before had been answered. Through Jacob, God had delivered his answer, not on my timetable but His own. Gratitude filled my heart. I wanted to hold on to Jacob and never let go because I knew he was a direct gift from God in answer to so many tearful prayers. For the first time, I saw myself living a full and happy life into old age, not cut short by suicide. Jacob had given me more than a ring; he had given me hope—hope for the future.

At length we left Alamo Plaza, walking a few blocks back to the River Walk. We settled down at Starbucks. We took turns calling family and friends on our cell phone to share the good news. The night was magical and special beyond expression.

Over the next six months, Jacob and I had many discussions about what our wedding should include… and exclude. We had similar ideas. Jacob was active in the decision-making process from the beginning and it made the preparations for the wedding that much more enjoyable. We decided from the beginning that we would make all the decisions together. We would accept suggestions from family and friends, but were clear that this wedding ceremony and celebration would only include the things that were precious and meaningful to us as a couple.

Having the opportunity to plan a second wedding was exciting. My first wedding was filled with the traditions and expectations of everyone else. This time around, I wanted to eliminate everything that held no significance to Jacob or me. We were able to sort through all the social requirements and keep only those of value to us.

The first major hurdle in planning a wedding was to find a location. At that point, my fiancé still attended Mass every Sunday, and I would reluctantly attend with him. Although we chose to worship there, the Catholic Mass still brought great pain and anxiety to me. We met with Father John, the parish priest, who more importantly was the priest who had recorded my story of abuse for the Catholic Church. He knew my history well by that time. I doubted that he could create a ceremony that was deeply spiritual, yet not religious. I left his office disillusioned. He couldn't see past the Catholic rules to envision a simple, sweet, Christ-based ceremony without the Mass.

At that point, we *both* left the Catholic Church. It couldn't meet our most basic need. We were wounded spiritually as a couple and needed a safe place to profess our love for one another in the presence of Christ. I vowed I would never set foot in a Catholic church again and to this day have honored that vow with the exception of my grandmother's funeral and one last visit with Father John as I was interviewing the characters in this book for their perspective. I believe Father John to be an honorable and holy man, but I do think he missed the forest because he was focused on the trees. This was difficult; both of our parents were devout Catholics. With the exception of the pool party incident in which I shared with my mother, Father Michael's intentions, our parents were not aware of my story. My mother had no conscious memory of the conversation during the pool party. They would not understand why we would choose a wedding outside the Catholic faith. Their disappointment would be real.

Jacob and I then began to consider all locations. We agreed that Jeremy, the hospice chaplain who had become my dear friend, would conduct the ceremony. We looked at every possible venue: hotels, museums, parks, botanical gardens, antebellum homes, backyards, etc. We settled on a beautiful chapel on Randolph Air Force Base. This old chapel was a replica of San José, the 'queen' of San Antonio's historic Franciscan missions. Because the chapel was not connected with any particular religion, we were free to develop a ceremony that would represent what mattered most to us without the restrictions or criteria of a particular denomination.

We now had chosen the location and the person who would perform the ceremony. We began to look at the details. The first and most important was our vows. We quickly decided that traditional wedding vows did not adequately communicate what we wanted to share with each other on that day. Together, we sat at Barnes and Nobles Bookstore and perused wedding books to get ideas on how to write our vows. We each wrote them together that day, contributing to each other's. We memorized them for the ceremony so there was none of that "repeat after me" nonsense. I feel compelled to share them here because they express the genuine love we have for each other.

Jacob: "I've been told I set my goals too high. I searched for someone who was honest, who could bring joy into my life, who would believe in me where others had doubts, accepting me for who I was, yet supportive of whom I wanted to become. I needed a special friend with whom I could share both laughter and tears; I needed a confidant who would be always ready to share my hopes, dreams, and secrets. I needed you.

Other times and other places are of no concern to me. I offer myself to a heart once broken. I promise honor and gentleness. I promise trust and confidence. I promise healing and love. My goal in life now is to be for you what I know you have become for me. And so on this day, before God and all these witnesses, I take you to be the wife of my days, the companion of my house, the friend of my life and the mother of my children. We shall bear together whatever trouble or sorrow life may lay upon us and we shall share together all the good and joyful things life may bring us. With these words, and all the words of my heart, I marry you and bind my life to yours."

Crystal: "I come this day to vow my love to one who is healer, believer and soul mate, who has reached to me from the crowd and offered a hand without condition; who has accepted my burdens and encircled me with love and gentleness. I shall always love you for choosing a gift once opened and making it new. You gave me trust when my heart would not return it, patience when I gave you fear, and softness when I thought my wounds would never heal. I pledge to you today a love I did not know was mine to give.

I give you strength of a companion who understands you and accepts you for who you are; I am the special friend with whom you can share both laughter and tears, the confidant who will uphold your hopes, dreams, and secrets. Finding and loving you has become the central event of my life, and so on this day, before God and all these witnesses, I take you to be the husband of my days, the companion of my house, the friend of my life and the father of our children. We shall bear together whatever trouble or sorrow life may lay upon us and we shall share together all the good and joyful things life may bring us. With these words, and all the words of my heart, I marry you and bind my life to yours."

Once the vows were written, we turned our attention to the various components of the ceremony. We liked the idea of having a traditional bridal party, but wanted to extend the concept a bit further. We had each sat through countless weddings where we could not identify the members of the bridal party or why each was significant to the bride and groom. Our wedding program wasn't just a list of names and a sequence of events; it told a story and featured each person in our bridal party as well as other key people who participated in our wedding day. In the program we spoke about how each person was special to us and why. We believed that people would enjoy hearing the story of how we met, so after the bridal party entered the chapel, we had a friend narrate the story of how we met through skating. Once the story was read, Jacob entered the church escorted by our friend, Velma, who was one of the two people who introduced us. Once Jacob approached the front of the chapel escorted down the center isle by Velma, I entered the church escorted by my skating coach, Lawrence, the second person involved in our introduction. We wanted to honor these two people for helping us meet.

Throughout our dating, Jacob and I would stop at fountains we found along our path. We each would pull out a penny, make a wish for each other; kiss the penny and then toss it into the fountain. We wanted to bring that sweet gesture into our wedding ceremony with participation from all of our guests. Toward the end of the ceremony, we approached the altar where a fountain was placed. We each held a penny from our birth year, made a wish… our prayer for each other, kissed it and tossed it in the fountain just as we had done so many times before. As the guests entered the banquet room for the reception, they passed a table with a fountain. A basket of pennies was placed next to the fountain along with a blank journal. We encouraged our guests to make a wish and write it in the journal. As a result, we have a beautiful journal with all our guests' well-wishes in it. Each anniversary, I pull out that book of wishes and re-visit the day through their kind words.

Focusing on all of these details seemed to distract me from my deep spiritual anguish. The work of therapy had exposed the raw pain deep within and even minor reminders of the Catholic faith caused anxiety. Guilt, shame and condemnation were still the predominant feelings provoked by faith, religion, God, and the Church. Being married in a church brought me great angst. I wasn't even aware that I was using the details of a wedding to shield me from the unprocessed injury of sexual abuse within the Catholic Church. However, I was very careful to exclude any reminder of that faith in our ceremony. This was the happiest time in my life and I knew I was marrying my soul mate without any hesitation or concern, yet I felt spiritually fragile and was apprehensive about the emotions a tender nuptial ceremony would evoke in me. I was searching for Grace and acceptance, but had not yet found it, and that lack left me feeling vulnerable and insecure about my relationship with God.

During the ceremony, my tears flowed freely. I was happy, without a doubt, but the tears became a cathartic release of years of pent up shame and guilt. I sobbed through the whole ceremony. It proved to be a healing moment in my life.

I can't write this story without addressing the impact the abuse had on my marriage and my relationship with my husband. I met him within weeks of reporting the abuse to the Church. Therapy had just gotten under way and my emotions were raw, since I was feeling things for the first time. Entering into a committed and loving relationship was frightening. I wasn't looking for a relationship and I wasn't sure if I was emotionally ready to enter one. Intimacy moved ever so slowly for us. We dated for six months before we kissed. I am amazed that my husband cared for me enough to be so patient and not rush. It gave us time to develop a true friendship. As our mutual trust increased, our intimacy grew, but not without tears, interruptions, moments of shame and humiliation, and the exercise of much patience... on both our parts. It was in these moments when the hardest part of the work took place. When tender moments of intimacy were replaced by shameful memories, the tears I cried came directly from my soul. I would cry with no reservation, much like a child.

It was a primal release of years of pent up shame and guilt. I cried for my mistakes, for interrupting the moment, for my childhood, but mostly, for the loss of joy and connectedness of an intimate relationship. I would attempt to restrain my tears during sex because I wanted Jacob to be satisfied and I knew tears of this kind would spoil the mood, but as soon as he finished, the dam broke and the tears fell. I would sob for hours without any explanation to my husband. He knew there were no words for my pain so he remained silent, but always present. In our early years, every sexual encounter ended in this way. I would eventually cry myself to sleep on his shoulder. There are no words to describe how tender and gentle this man was and continues to be with me. During these moments of raw, exposed grief, my tears became my silent prayers. I could not even form the thoughts, but I always felt God's presence, much like my husband's… silent, but loving.

As our relationship grew and strengthened, we learned ways to avoid those moments of intense pain. Over time, we have replaced those shameful memories with new, pleasant ones. Occasionally, pain will again invade our bedroom unannounced and uninvited. I have learned to listen to myself and if I am feeling fragile or vulnerable, I avoid sexual intimacy. I know not to engage in sex with my husband if I have just gotten off an airplane where I sat next to a priest for the afternoon. There are still triggers and I suppose there will always be, but I have learned to manage them.

Chapter 14: Mother Hurt

Despite all the pain of a sexual relationship, there was enough love to conceive a child, but pregnancy brought a new set of challenges and fears. When we first found out we were pregnant, we were ecstatic. I could only think of the love in my heart that I would share, and the chance to correct generations of mistakes, but the joy didn't last long. As a nurse, I knew what would occur during the pre-natal physician's visits as well as during the delivery. Anxiety poured over me and I was ready to get an abortion just to avoid the trauma of delivery... and yes, I understand how irrational that sounds, but that was my state of mind at the time.

My husband and I started watching the birthing shows on television, and that sent me into hysterics. As I watched the women on television give birth, I was acutely aware of the number of people in the room all gaping at their genitals! I begged my husband and my physician to use general anesthesia to deliver my baby. I didn't want any part of it. I requested a caesarean section to avoid a vaginal delivery, but my physician refused. I had never shared my past with my obstetrician, even though she had seen me since I was 18 years old. On every visit, my face and chest was blotchy and red. I couldn't hide my anxiety. In my third trimester, with my husband present, I shared my story with her and begged her for surgery. She still declined, but did offer to induce labor to ensure that she would deliver and I wouldn't have to endure a strange person.

We also discussed the number of people required in the room for delivery and decided that the bare minimum was three people besides my husband… the physician, a nurse for me and a nurse for the baby. Normally, more staff is present, but she would ensure that only those three would attend. I was not comfortable with her assurances, but I had to accept them. I even begged my husband to deliver at home. He was a physician; I was a nurse; we could make it work. He lovingly reminded me he was an oral surgeon and although he had exposure to labor and delivery, he wasn't prepared to deliver his own child. I know I was being unreasonable, but I was looking for a way to escape those feelings of shame and humiliation that paralyzed me. I finally accepted what I must do. My backup plan was to zone out as I had learned to do all those years before. How sad! I was planning to zone out on the birth of my first daughter! I wasn't thinking about her or her health, just my overwhelming shame. These are the moments of joy that the abuse stole from my life.

The delivery was arranged. I would arrive at the hospital on April 17th for a planned induction. Only, my daughter had a different idea. She decided to arrive 17 days earlier than her due date. After a dinner date with my husband, we returned home and as I climbed into bed for the night, my water broke with no warning. I had no contractions, but I knew there was cause for concern because there was meconium in the fluid. Meconium is the baby's first stool. It is not normal for a fetus to release meconium in utero unless there is distress. We both knew there was cause for concern and I also knew the delivery was inevitable. My physician was out of town. I did not know the physician on call. I reluctantly went to the hospital.

The hospital staff was discreet, gracious and very gentle. It made long labor—of seventeen hours—easier. The labor wasn't what I was anxious about. My anxiety could not have been higher when the physician came in to check me and found meconium all over the sheets. The Neonatal Intensive Care Staff, Neonatalogists, Respiratory Therapy, Lab Techs and about ten other staff immediately rushed in my room. To make matters worse it was three o'clock in the afternoon: shift change for the nurses. I couldn't believe I was getting a new nurse at that crucial point. The day shift nurse chose to stay with me as well. I was grateful because we had built a nice rapport, but that meant another person in the room.

My daughter had her umbilical cord wrapped around her neck twice and was in immediate jeopardy. It was time to push and I was so overwhelmed with all the people in the room I couldn't focus. I turned to my husband and started to cry, begging them to leave the room. My daughter was in real trouble and I couldn't focus on that because I was so traumatized by the number of people present. I saw the look in the physician's eyes when she told me I had to push--*now*. I knew if I did not, there was a very real possibility my daughter would be damaged. At that moment, I felt the maternal instinct take charge, despite what was going on inside and around me.

Luckily, I didn't have to push for long. After one hour, my daughter was born, blue, but eventually okay. I missed the opportunity to hold her right after delivery, which I'm sure, would have made all the anxiety worth it. She was taken immediately to the NICU. My husband accompanied her at my request. I was left to process all that had just happened. I cried to the point of exhaustion and welcomed sleep.

My fear of formalized religion did not negate the need to have my daughter baptized into the Christian faith. I knew entering into a church would make the day more about the hurt in my heart than about the Christening of my first born. I would not have enjoyed the ceremony, and probably would have been emotionally unavailable. Instead, my husband and I opted for a baptismal ceremony in the natural environment of a park. We created a ceremony that included our dearest family and friends, not just as spectators, but as active participants in this celebration. We encouraged everyone to wear shorts and bring swimsuits, because we had planned a day of fun and celebration around our daughter's christening.

The ceremony was performed under a rented canopy with all of our family and friends circled around us. Each guest participated by reading *The Twelve Gifts of Birth.* After Jeremy baptized her by pouring water over her head, everyone had the opportunity to bless our daughter, Lauren, with the sign of the cross as the sweetest lullaby played in the background. It was tender and intimate and held far more meaning than any canned Baptism would have been in a church ceremony. My daughter wore a simple, antique white linen christening gown that had been worn by at least three generations in my family. Much like our wedding, significant meaning and purpose filled every detail. At the conclusion of the ceremony, we continued our celebration with a huge, catered picnic, a tournament of horseshoes, swimming, and the best fellowship that family and friends could offer. Christ manifested His presence throughout that day. He clearly was not waiting for us to show up in church. The blessed day ended, and for me, a moment of Grace touched my life.

My second daughter arrived two years after Lauren. By this time, the hard work in therapy had started to pay off. Emotionally, I was in a better place. Anxiety did not penetrate my being during the second pregnancy. I wasn't trying to avoid the impending birth. Ironically, we were on our way to our friends' infant funeral when I went into labor. Labor progressed quickly and instead of going to the funeral, we went straight to the hospital. By the time I arrived at the hospital, pain prevented me from walking during the contractions. There was no time to be anxious or think about anything else except the pain of the contractions. I delivered Emily just a couple of hours after arriving to the hospital. Her birth, although more physically painful than Lauren's was sweeter because I could stay present and enjoy my precious little gift from above.

Chapter 15: Searching For a Church Home

The birth of my first daughter prompted my husband and me to try a church again. He had always been ready and had missed attending church on a regular basis, but chose to remain home with me instead. He never voiced concern or complaint about not attending, but when asked, he acknowledged his desire to go. During our journey together, he lost his confidence in his religion too. He was not looking to change religions or even to stop attending church services altogether. He had been comfortable with the Catholic faith, but his choice to accompany me on this spiritual odyssey caused him to question the very institution he had grown to love.

Although I always felt guilty over not attending church, the pressure became intolerable once our daughters were born. I was now a mother and it wasn't all about me anymore. I had a responsibility to educate and nurture my children's faith in Christ despite the injustice I had suffered. I was not prepared to return to the Catholic Church, but if not Catholic, then what? I had never even attended a different kind of worship and was always made to feel that it was a sin to do so as if Catholics were the only true Christians worthy of grace and admittance into heaven.

Months passed with this problem heavy on my heart. Each week I would tell my husband that I was ready to try church again, but as Sunday morning came, I couldn't go. I was scared—of the unknown, scared of my reaction, but mostly scared that I might introduce my girls to something that would harm them in the worst way.

At the same time, I ran into my best friend from my childhood, who invited me to a M.O.P.S. group at a local Lutheran Church. This organization is devoted to the Christian fellowship of Mothers of Pre-Schoolers. They met twice a month, shared a meal, listened to guest speakers and did crafts. This seemed non-threatening and a great way to meet other women with small children. I thoroughly enjoyed the time with M.O.P.S. and it was the connection I needed to find the courage to walk into a church again. Many of the women who attended the meetings were members of the Lutheran church and always talked about how much they were spiritually fed there. The monthly meetings allowed me to become comfortable with the church campus and physical surroundings.

My concerns seem less than earth-shaking, but when my husband and I walked through the doors of the church, it didn't feel foreign, and for me, especially, that was vitally important. By the time we attended our first Sunday service, I had come to know the caregivers in the church nursery quite well. I trusted them and felt my children were safe. My husband and I instantly liked the pastor and the music. For the first month, I still sat in the pew and cried with my husband's arm around me, but for the first time in years, I felt my spirit come alive. I was able to hear and absorb the message of God's Grace in a way that I could never have done before.

I had always felt dammed to Hell no matter what good works and kind spirit I brought to the world, but the message in this church was different and fulfilling. It healed the wound in my heart and allowed forgiveness to enter. It made me want to be a better person and it was here that the seeds of doing something powerful with this story began. I was quite aware that this church belonged to a denomination with a hierarchy, rules and politics, but here I was able to separate the message of God's grace from the administrative organization. I was able to see the pastor as a simple man with a wife and four kids struggling to survive like everyone else. When speaking, his attitude was never 'you are sinners'; it was always 'we are sinners.' He never represented himself as infallible and there was no celibacy issue. The church building had a large cross hanging behind the altar, but with no corpus. This was significant for me because each time I saw a crucifix with the corpus, I associated it with the ones I had seen all those years hanging on the wall in the rectory, stored in the office, or lying on Father Michael's bed. It never represented God's Grace and sacrifice. It always represented my sin that could never be forgiven. It said to me, *Look what Christ did for you and this is how you repay him.* Those were the tapes that played in my mind each time I saw Christ's body on the cross.

The Lutheran Church offered features of the liturgy that we had found valuable and precious in the Catholic rite: communion, profession of faith and scriptural readings. It was similar enough to be familiar and comfortable, but different enough to not evoke anxiety. It was a good fit. Throughout my struggles with religion and spirituality, the one profession that I have held onto was the Apostle's Creed. I could take that creed and read it word for word and know that was my faith. There were no man-made rules in it; just a statement of what I believed to be true. When all else in my spiritual world seemed lost, I would turn to the Creed and feel at peace. I wasn't sophisticated in my knowledge of the Bible, but the Creed comforted me through many long, agonized nights. When abuse and religion blurred together and I couldn't distinguish what was true and real from what was not, the Creed gave me clarity. To this day, I feel I am in my infancy in learning about God's grace and purpose for my life, but throughout all my life, I have never doubted that God exists. There were times when I couldn't feel His love, especially in those moments when suicide seemed so comforting, but I knew He was always there. Many times suicide seemed like such an attractive option, not to escape the pain I was in, but to move toward the love He offered. At last, I know how irrational that was.

Chapter 16: A Plan to Give Back

An overwhelming desire began weighing on my heart, to volunteer my gifts and talents and give back to an organization, institution or program that could truly use me. With my husband struggling to complete a grueling, six-year residency in Oral and Maxillofacial Surgery, and me working doubly hard to ensure that the tasks of the day were accomplished, I did not have any energy to give even a tiny portion of my time to anyone other than my two small girls and my husband. I was physically and emotionally exhausted just keeping up with that. But, even through the exhaustion, I kept hearing one of those 'God whispers' that told me I had something significant to offer the world.

Once I had recovered from the trauma in my life and my husband had graduated from the residency program, our family moved to O'Fallon, Illinois near the dynamic city of St. Louis. My husband's schedule had slowed to a pace that enabled him to participate in the care of our two girls and help with the chores around the house. The 'God whisper' grew stronger in me. I now had the emotional and physical energy to contribute to society in other ways than just raising two girls to become productive members of society. I spent many evenings on my new front porch in the rocking chair considering how my gifts and abilities could best be used. I considered foster parenting, becoming a hospice or humane society volunteer, but none of those options answered the 'God whisper' growing louder every day.

While talking with my dear friend, Jeremy, the same hospice chaplain who encouraged me to report the sexual abuse to the Catholic Church, the 'God whisper' became clear. He had often told me that I should become a teacher because I was effective and clear in those presentations for hospice where he had heard me speak. In that moment, I knew what I wanted: to provide inspirational speaking for an audience that could hear the message of struggle, depression, abuse and in the end, would hear, above all else, the tremendous power of God's Grace.

Now that I knew what I wanted to do and what message I wanted to deliver, I had to determine who my audience would be. I understood that my life story was problematic and the subject matter wouldn't be appropriate in every context. Then it dawned on me: Why not offer my services to the one place that needs to hear it the most... the Catholic Church itself? I didn't want to blame the institution; I wanted to enlighten it through my experience and to share my story with its people, hoping that I could provide sexual abuse awareness training for all employees in the Catholic diocese. I was skeptical that my offer would be accepted and actually come to fruition, but I knew my responsibility was to *offer* the service. I could not make them accept it or utilize it, but I could provide another option to consider.

Without wasting any time, I called the local diocese and requested to speak with the person who handled complaints of sexual abuse within the church. My phone call was forwarded to a lovely woman whose role was to receive any complaints or accusations from the community and to become a liaison for the person filing the complaint. I explained a little about my vision and she offered to meet with me for further discussion. She gave me the option of meeting at the chancery or at a location of my choosing. Instantly, my hopes grew. Not only because she didn't shut me down without serious consideration, but also I could tell the recent national scandal had changed the way in which the church was now handling this problem. It was comforting to know that persons needing to file a complaint no longer had to confront a priest or nun and no longer had to travel to the 'lion's den,' the chancery or other church office to share their story.

I agreed to meet Lindsay at the chancery. This decision may seem perplexing, but I wanted to show Lindsay that I had arrived at an emotional, spiritual, and psychological level where meeting her in the 'lion's den' was comfortable. It was my way of demonstrating to her that I had done the work necessary to process the entire gamut of emotions and could now meet her in a place that would have once caused immense anxiety. It was an attempt to reassure her that I had the emotional courage and psychological sophistication to follow through on what I was offering. This gesture laid the foundation for me to demonstrate that my intentions were not ill-designed. I wanted to reassure her that my purpose was to offer training and education in any way that could be helpful.

Despite the firm purpose behind my decision, I walked to the chancery office with my stomach rising toward my throat and my gut swirling with anxiety. I remembered my mantra from years before: *put one foot in front of the other, keep going.* The chancery office was located in an old, red brick building. The wooden floors creaked as I entered the squeaking door. I introduced myself to the receptionist tucked in the corner of the tiny lobby and explained that I had scheduled a meeting with Lindsay. She invited me to sit down. As I sat, I could hear water swishing through the plumbing as someone used the restroom. The stale smell reminded me of an old person's house. I'm not exactly sure what that smell is, but it typified many homes I visited as a hospice nurse and it was familiar. As I lifted my eyes from my knees, I noticed the tale-tell signs of Catholicism… the ever-present crucifix hanging on the wall, statues of saints standing in the corners, a rosary placed on the corner of the desk and a Bible on the end table. My mind raced back to the rectory where Father Michael had lived and I began to think, *What am I doing here?* Just then, Lindsay walked in and I was relieved. Lindsay was about my age and I felt instantly connected to her. I could tell she had a genuine desire to improve the training and awareness within the Church and was excited about what I could offer.

She led me into a large, old conference room. The antique furniture smelled musty. As I glanced around the room, I noticed, once again, the ever-present crucifix along with an almost life-size statue of the Virgin Mary. My anxiety increased as I took a seat in one of the chairs around the conference table. I sat on my hands to keep from fidgeting. Lindsay was ultra guarded in her approach, but as we talked, we both relaxed. I gave her a brief synopsis of my history and then began to explain my vision of speaking to groups about my experience in a positive and uplifting way. Her eyes glowed with excitement. She had many ideas to share with me and confessed that she had been looking for a victim who would be willing to share her experience. Together, we came up with four groups of people that could benefit from my story.

The first group of people was the one Lindsay was most excited about. She was in the process of developing mandatory training on the subject of child abuse upon hire and annually thereafter for all employees and volunteers. She believed my story had especial value for this group of people.

My focus was on the second group identified—the diocesan priests working in the various parishes. I wanted them to see, in real life, the brokenness caused by sexual abuse. Lindsay accepted this idea also, but with a different focus. She explained that many of the diocesan priests reluctantly attended the mandatory training because they felt it didn't pertain to them. Many of them were just as shocked as the rest of the world when a priest was accused of sexually inappropriate behavior. She told me they were embarrassed and ashamed and many of them were concerned that when seen in public, people were silently wondering if they had been sexually abusive with children. It put an invisible 'bulls-eye' on their forehead. Lindsay believed my story would enlighten the priests who felt the subject didn't pertain to them, and perhaps, soften their hearts. She felt that for the priests who were saddened by the overwhelming accusations of abuse against the church, it would provide a different perspective. After all, the priests accused of abuse and removed from the church were often friends and colleagues of the ones who now had to take courses on child abuse awareness. Lindsay described these priests as the second victims in the ordeal because the friends and colleagues they thought they knew had a secret life. I agreed to that focus, but in my head I couldn't see the value of my story for them, since I was the enemy, the cause of their disgrace.

The third group of people to benefit from my story was junior high and high school students. I loved this idea because I think there is a powerful message in learning to follow your gut instinct… those God whispers. I knew that group of people would require great finesse on my part. Sexual abuse is a taboo subject and people at that age have many different levels of understanding.

The last group of people identified came from a suggestion from my dear friend, Jeremy. Seminary students were the perfect audience and could benefit the most. My story could expose them to potential problems they might encounter and the consequences of those problems. It could also teach them how to handle a situation should someone choose to disclose an abusive situation to them, regardless if the one being accused were affiliated with the church or not.

Lindsay concluded our meeting by explaining that all of these ideas and plans would need to be brought to the Vicar General so that he could, in turn, bring them to the Bishop for ultimate approval. The Bishop had only been in his job for less than a week, so time was needed for him to acquaint himself with his new staff and responsibilities. I acknowledged the hierarchy and left very hopeful.

Prior to my departure, Lindsay asked if I would put together a small biography so that she could share with the Vicar General and Bishop. I agreed and the one page biography I prepared for her became the seed to start this book. Early in high school, I had fleeting moments of dreaming of becoming a writer. I journaled on a daily basis, knowing in my heart that this story would one day be born.

After a few follow-up phone calls to Lindsay, it became evident that the church was not in a place to follow through with the ideas we discussed. Lindsay remained hopeful and encouraging to me, but between her words I sensed that those ideas would never come to fruition.

Chapter 17: Kimberley

During the days when my marriage with Charles was collapsing, and when I started to work in the hospice industry, I met my best friend, Kimberley. She had joined the hospice where I worked and we became instant friends. The connection Kimberley and I shared was unlike any other relationship I had experienced. With her, I could be myself. I could say anything to her without having to weigh my words. We spent our weekends shopping and eating. She represented the fun in my life and as time went by, that fun never faded. We would go to an all-you-can-eat buffet and only eat the dessert… one of everything! We would giggle over the sinful and carefree idea of eating only pie for dinner. We would go shopping for clothes and never think twice about sharing a dressing room as we tried them on. Often we left with exactly the same articles of clothing. We would laugh for hours at how silly many of the things we tried on looked. She often would spend the night; we would get up late in the morning to a casual cup of coffee, more gossip and more shopping before she started on the hour and a half journey that took her home.

Early in our friendship, we traveled to Cancun and Cozumel together, creating one of the best memories of my life. We sat on the street corner in Cozumel after a day of snorkeling, smoking Swisher Sweet cigars with our hair matted from the sea water. When we arrived at our room, exhausted, filthy, but very hungry, we ordered a full lobster dinner to feast on in our room. We rented four-wheelers and went riding in our swimsuits through the Mexican jungle, stopping to jump into the icy waters of a hidden cenote, a natural sink hole, filled with pristine water. We were covered in mud at the end, but what a ride! We explored Mayan ruins, crawled through undeveloped caves with only a flashlight and played bumper cars with the vehicles. What a blast!

Kimberley joined me for the drive to various skating competitions. We were in Waco, Texas for a regional competition. I had a break in my events so we decided to do a little sight-seeing. There isn't much in Waco, but one of our funniest memories comes from there. After visiting a museum, we got into my white Honda Accord and started to drive through the downtown streets. Unbeknownst to us, when I made a left-hand turn, we entered a parade route. It was June nineteenth, Juneteenth, the celebration of the Emancipation Proclamation. We were the only two Caucasian people in the parade. So, we rolled our windows down and started to wave as if our participation had been planned from the conception of the celebration. Two white girls, a white car, and a Juneteenth parade: that is what a classic Kimberley/Crystal memory looks like!

On that same trip, as we traveled, we were stopped by a traffic jam caused by a car accident. There was a lengthy delay as traffic sat parked on the interstate for more than an hour. That placed me in danger of not being able to skate. I might miss my first event. To make up time, we decided not to stop for bathroom breaks along the way. As we neared the city, I desperately had to urinate. The only option was a used, fast-food drink cup. Yet again, another Kimberley/Crystal memory was about to be made. I placed the cup on the floorboard of the passenger side. I turned my body around so that my back was leaning against the dashboard. I lowered my pants and voided, all the while laughing at the ridiculous situation. That memory surfaces every time I see or use one of those drink cups. You can only allow yourself to be that vulnerable with someone you completely trust: your best friend.

Many of my most poignant memories include Kimberley. She was Maid of Honor at my marriage to Jacob. She drove in from her home an hour and a half away at a moment's notice to support and encourage me during the long hours of labor with both my girls. She celebrated and cried as both of our daughters were born. At each girl's Baptism, she honored us by serving as Godmother.

Years later, as I was preparing to move with my family to St. Louis, Kimberley and I spent a weekend in Las Vegas. What a weekend we had! I was still nursing my second daughter, so I had to stop frequently to express the excess milk from my breasts. Together, we sat on Las Vegas Boulevard at Jimmy Buffet's Margaritaville as I discreetly pumped the milk from my breast. We laughed at the reaction of the passersby who were curious, but didn't want to look. Time with Kimberley was care and worry free. We did things just to be silly and spontaneous. We went out of our way to make memories. This was the time when I made up for the happiness I had missed in my childhood, but with the privileges and wisdom of an adult.

When we left San Antonio, Kimberley accompanied us on the two-day drive to St. Louis, with two babies, a husband, and a cat. She volunteered to baby sit our girls so that Jacob and I could have date nights, a tremendous and frequent gift. During this entire friendship, she stood by my side as I confronted the sexual abuse I had endured. She supported me with carefree adventures at a time when there was much pain and sadness during therapy. Since she had grown up as the daughter of a Methodist minister, Kimberley could engage in spiritual and biblical conversations that helped me redefine my initial understanding of the Christian faith taught by Father Michael. When the pain of therapy became more than I could bear, she could ease the tension with a day of shopping and fun. Our friendship has stood the test of time, I look forward to growing old with her and reminiscing about all the crazy and wild things we shared.

Chapter 18: Jeremy

I have neglected to reveal just how vital a role Jeremy, my dear friend, played in this journey of mine. His presence in my life cannot be valued highly enough. In the beginning, he brought to painful life those feelings about my past that I kept suppressed, muted and numb. His accent, his mannerisms, his word choices, even his shoes reminded me of Father Michael, a man that I associated with anxiety, shame and guilt. Each encounter with Jeremy brought out those same feelings in me.

How did I ever see beyond that similarity to Father Michael to accept Jeremy as one of the dearest, truest friends, one I have come to love? We worked side-by-side in hospice for six years, during the time I was in therapy. To keep those reminders from becoming too upsetting, I set certain ground rules for him. First, he had to ditch the 'priest' shoes, those black leather loafers every priest I had ever seen wore. Second, he couldn't leave me messages by voice mail. I could not differentiate between his voice and Father Michael's on a taped message. Each time he would leave me a message, I felt my stomach drop and my hands begin to shake from adrenaline. I knew it made no sense for Father Michael to leave a message, but my first assumption was that Michael was calling.

The third area caused the greatest anxiety and always left me nauseated and on the brink of vomiting. When Jeremy prayed out loud with patients and families, he would soften his voice and lower it by an octave. This voice change mirrored the tone and quality of Father Michael's prayers. I may have been physically present with those patients and families, but emotionally and spiritually I was disengaged and 'checked-out.' If I could, I would excuse myself during times of prayer to avoid the unpleasant feelings sure to arise. When it came time for my wedding, I wanted Jeremy to perform it, but had multiple conversations with him about how he should approach prayer during the ceremony.

Once the rules were established, our friendship grew. I continued my work in therapy and as I discovered just how shattered was my image of a priest and ultimately of God, Jeremy became the counterbalance. I viewed Jeremy as a gentle, honorable man with great integrity. Because of his experience as a priest who chose to leave the priesthood, I could compare his choices with those of Father Michael. Knowing Jeremy put a human face on an otherwise God-like religious leader. I saw Jeremy as a man; a man with wants, needs, and desires. My view of priests never included such human qualities and it worked as a reality check for me to see them in Jeremy. Each step along the way, I would compare Father Michael's behavior to my dear friend Jeremy's, who modeled what Christ-like meant better than anyone I had ever met.

There was always, and continues to be, a subtle dance that occurs in our relationship. Only recently have I been able to discuss the details of the abuse openly with him. With Jeremy, there is a constant and permanent association to the abuse I endured... because he's Irish, because he's an ex-priest, because he gave me strength and urged me to report the abuse and seek therapy, and because he wore those black 'priest shoes'! When you are ashamed and depressed, you tend to hang your head instead of holding it high with confidence. When I looked down out of shame, it was those same 'priest shoes' that I'd seen all those years before. Despite all that, our friendship has grown stronger with each passing year. Not only did he perform the marriage ceremony for me and my husband, he baptized our first daughter at a time when attending church gave more pain that comfort. As our relationship grew, he and his wife honored our family by becoming the Godparents of our second daughter.

Chapter 19: Finding Grace

My twenties were filled with anger and disappointment toward my mother. I placed all the blame for the abuse on her. I did not direct my anger toward Father Michael or the church. Projecting my anger onto my mother proved to be a safer alternative. Anger and blame directed at Father Michael or the church appeared to be confronting God about the injustice I suffered. Raised a Catholic, I was taught never to challenge God, church law, priests or any adult figure. That explains my unwillingness to express anger toward such an august institution. My mother, on the other hand, well, was my mother. What safer person was there? Throughout this entire time, my parents were completely oblivious to what was happening during my visits with Father Michael. I kept my secret from them for years.

As each year passed, my anger grew and I blamed them more. I couldn't forgive them for not protecting me and not giving me what I needed in the first place. As far as I was concerned, it wasn't Father Michael who was to blame; they were, especially my mother for not nurturing me emotionally. All of this anger came to a boiling point one day during a phone conversation with her. We were talking about religion, debating the role of the Catholic Church in each of our spiritual journeys. The conversation was tense and loaded with bad feeling. As it continued, my anxiety and anger grew. I blurted out what her religion had cost me. I told her that Father Michael had sexually abused me for years. The way it came out was mean, piercing, and vengeful. I threw all the blame, frustration, and pain directly at her and didn't try to rescue her from her devastation. For once, I refused to acknowledge my mother's shortcomings and placed the blame in her lap. Today, I deeply regret that conversation; I was cruel. Much remains unsaid about that conversation and the topic of sexual abuse. It is not open for discussion. I think we both would like it to be, but it is charged with so much pain and anxiety that neither of us is able to go there.

My mother remains responsible for not advocating for me when she had suspicions, concerns and doubts regarding Father Michael's keen interest in me. But she surely didn't deserve to be blamed for choices Father Michael made or for the Church's insensitive response to my allegation. Life's lessons can be quite painful. I learned compassion that day by being the opposite. I will not make that mistake again in my life. My mother did not deserve my spitefulness that day, even if it did clear the air. I have since learned to allow her to express her feelings without taking responsibility for them, while offering her my love and support.

Only in becoming a mother myself, have I realized that I placed on my mother an unfair burden of responsibility for the injuries suffered from a sophisticated and subtle attack on my sexuality and spiritual development. Although my mother is not psychologically sophisticated, she was aware of the turmoil that darkened my life. I did not allow her the opportunity of insight and understanding since I chose not to include her. She has been troubled throughout our journey together, knowing that she only knew my outer shell. Her attempt at cracking that shell never ceased and because of her tenacity, she has become the most wonderful grandmother any child could ask for. I watch her re-write history, correcting her mistakes through my children. These moments of Grace have redefined my relationship with her. My heart smiles as I watch her read story after story to my children, or watch her consent to my daughter's incessant demands to scratch her back. She spends hours at the table coloring with them when she doubtless needs to be tending to other things instead. My daughters run to her like water to a sponge and I watch her soak up all the love, knowing that we are both growing and learning in this game called life.

Even though I understand the disproportion of blame toward my mother, I still can't summon the courage to become out-of-control-teeth-gritting furious at the mere man who caused so much damage. I want to scream at the top of my lungs at all the ways his actions stifled or outright halted my development. After the screaming, I want to collapse in a huddle on the floor and weep to the point of exhaustion, but in fact, I can't summon those natural emotions within me despite desperately wanting to do so.

I loved Father Michael at a time when I felt unlovable. I depended on his guidance and his encouraging and uplifting words. Even though I can fully acknowledge all the pain and confusion he caused, I can also still hear the encouraging and calming words he spoke in moments when the temptation of suicide clouded my thoughts and judgment. How can I be out-of-control furious at a man whose words may have saved my life? His words may have saved not only my life, but spared my parents and all who knew and loved me the indescribable grief my suicide would have caused them.

I have to accept the idea that all people make good and bad choices. I will choose to defend the good choices Father Michael made despite living through the consequences of his wrong ones. If I do not, grief, anger and disappointment will consume me and halt the progress I have made on my spiritual journey.

The past two years have been the most peaceful of my life. I love my husband with all my heart. I have two beautiful little girls. During all my years as a Catholic, I never understood the meaning of Grace. I was raised to believe that you had to earn your way to heaven. I spent years searching for Grace in everything but myself. I never once thought to look within. I remained empty-handed when everywhere I looked failed to bring relief to the unforgiving, relentless pain that left me feeling isolated, alone and completely abandoned.

To discover that Grace was a gift from God was a completely new concept for me. I always knew that Christ died for my sins, but I didn't understand that I was destined to sin. No matter how hard I tried, I would always fall short. God knew that and sent His son to remedy our brokenness. It doesn't matter what choices I made in the past or the reason behind each choice. What matters is that a loving God gave the gift of His son to me and everyone who believes in Him. I am safe, forgiven, accepted and loved.

I no longer have to struggle with guilt that I am not worthy. It was in that moment of insight that I forgave myself; the years of guilt, humiliation and shame melted away. It was such a special and awe-inspiring moment that I named my second daughter Emily Grace for the Grace I felt. Finding Grace has been the single most important Gift in my life. It makes the old hymn "Amazing Grace" real and true for me. "I once was lost, but now am found." It is the Grace within each of us that touches the most tender and dearest part of our spirit. Grace isn't something dangling just out of reach like a carrot to a horse, but is found within each person. Grace shines out of others who touch and bless us when we are unaware. Grace sustains us when we cannot sustain ourselves. It bubbles up from within at times when the soft God whisper is needed. God gently delivers His Grace through the encouragement of family and friends. Grace brushes us in moments of everyday life from people close to us, and even from strangers we meet. Grace is the person who interrupts a busy moment to hold open the door for a few more seconds so you may pass with ease. Grace is the person who adds extra dollars to a waitress' tip, not because she did an exceptional job, but because her job is difficult and brings little reward. Grace is the one extra bedtime story read to a child, despite the parent's fatigue. Grace is the love of a husband who ignores the baby weight never lost by his wife. Examples of Grace can be found in every moment, if only we are open to see it, hear it, and feel it. My challenge now is to deliver that message in a clear and loving way to my beautiful girls.

I was sitting in church one day listening to the pastor's weekly sermon, and an epiphany came to me. The sermon revolved around the Scriptural passage about a prostitute caught in the act of adultery and on the brink of death by stoning. The religious leaders wanted to challenge Jesus' teachings by questioning him whether the woman should be stoned to death or not. Jesus' brilliant response neither condoned nor condemned. He said, "Let whoever is without sin cast the first stone." The 'ah-hah' moment occurred with me. For the first time, I understood the truth that this wonderful gift of Grace that I received wasn't just for me. That same Grace is offered to Father Michael without hesitation, for that is the beauty and whole purpose of Christ's death on the cross… so that *all* of our sins can be washed away. Grace was Father Michael's gift and he was no less worthy of God's Grace than I was. This revelation just added to my healing and ultimate ability to forgive him, the Church, and me. I felt as if I had just taken a huge leap in my spiritual journey.

As for the Catholic Church, my anger toward it has melted away somehow. I am cautious, but understand that there are many good and holy people within that institution. Many of my dearest family and friends share the Catholic faith and I see on a daily basis the peace, strength and courage it provides for them. I honor and respect that and I have offered the Church my story as a small solution to the very big problem it faces.

Chapter 20: A Change of Heart

The question remains, though, would Father Michael accept that gift through acknowledgement of his own sins? I will never know that answer, and do admit that I frequently wonder whether he is aware of the hurt he caused.

I often play tapes in my head how the conversation would go if I ever had the opportunity to speak with him. I have long believed that this is a missing element of my healing. I want closure... closure on our friendship, closure on the manipulation and abuse, and closure in knowing that I can and do offer him complete and unconditional forgiveness. What if a conversation with Father Michael could bring *him* peace? What if he had carried his sorrow with him all these years because he was not allowed to contact me to apologize? There is enough forgiveness in me to offer him a conversation that could be equally healing for both of us.

On the other hand, what if he is stuck in the same destructive and abusive thought patterns as the day he left my life? What if he is angry and bitter that I destroyed a successful career? I can't know how I would feel if any of those questions were answered, but I do know that if I leave that conversation unspoken, I will grow to be an old lady with a huge piece of unfinished business haunting my final years.

In my years of working with hospice patients I learned that if people cannot or refuse to deal with raw issues, those issues don't go away over time. In fact, they tend to manifest themselves in a physical form at the end of life. Terminal restlessness is heart-breaking to watch as a person suffers through it. It often mimics the panicked anxiety of being suffocated. At that point, it is too late to work through unresolved pain as impending death looms near.

Let me share a very real experience I had with one of my patients. She was quite elderly, nearly one-hundred years of age. She was actively dying. Despite being only hours from death, she remained cognizant. Her pain escalated out of control. With the physician's help, we tried every medication and treatment available, and yet her pain would not subside.

The active dying stage that usually takes hours became days. She couldn't die because she was in too much pain. Dying requires a relaxation of all muscles while severe pain forces the muscles to contract. Having exhausted all medical possibilities, I asked our hospice chaplain to step in. I wanted her to explore the idea that perhaps it was spiritual pain manifesting itself in a physiological form. The chaplain spent an entire day with this woman. At the end of the day the patient had died peacefully with the chaplain at her bedside.

When the chaplain arrived back at our office, I asked her what she had said that helped the lady relax and let go. She explained that as she sat with that sweet woman, the lady shared a childhood story with her. When she was a young child, her family had gone on a camping trip. During that trip, her older sister held her down while her older brother raped her. Both her older brother and older sister had since died and she was afraid of meeting them after death. I'm not sure what the chaplain said to calm her, but at the end of the day, she was able to let go of that fear and die peacefully. Perhaps she taught the dying woman how to forgive.

I could easily see myself in that patient's predicament. I want to resolve my pain in this lifetime and certainly don't want to linger for days because I am afraid to meet Father Michael on the other side of death. Regardless of the outcome, a conversation with him would give me closure. At the very least, it would open the door to more healing and growth.

I would also look for forgiveness from him. Even though I was an adolescent during that time, I played a part with the decisions I made. Although I realize many people will not understand this, I know that by reporting the abuse to the Church, Father Michael lost a vibrant and successful career. His missions were booked months in advance and many parishes enjoyed his ministry so much that he was asked back year after year. I want to talk with him, to learn how his loss affected him and what happened in the following months and years. Perhaps, when he returned to Ireland, he re-entered the career he left in the States. Perhaps he was never allowed to function as a priest again. I just don't know. I would want to share with him my journey, the healing, the heartache, and the challenges. I want him to read this book and reflect on the message in it.

The logistics of contacting Father Michael may prove to be very complex. The only contact I have is with the Provincial's office in Dublin. I'm not sure how eager they would be to facilitate that meeting. If Father Michael was no longer associated with the priesthood, they might not know his current location. Also, too, years have passed; he is an old man now and could even be dead. I'm not sure the opportunity still exists for those conversations to happen; the window may have already closed.

If all the challenges of locating him were resolved, what would that meeting look like? Would I travel to Europe; would it be a telephone call, a letter? A face-to-face meeting would obviously cause the greatest anxiety. I keep fantasizing how that initial greeting would be. Would we shake hands, hug, or not touch at all? If we did shake hands, would his touch send me into an anxiety attack so severe that nothing could be accomplished? Would I get to that point and then not even be able to speak?

The emotional process of writing this book has spurred me to find the answers to these questions. So, after of years of wanting no contact with Father Michael, I am now ready to open the doors of communication with him. I have had a change of heart. Going through the process of articulating my life's journey has made me realize that it is one-sided. Each person I portray in this book may have a different view of the events. I have spoken with each one to learn their interpretation of the events described here. I have gained great insight from their perspectives. Father Michael remains the one person I cannot reach. I can only assume his side of the story would be just as gripping. I am ready to hear his version of the story, as well as how his time with me impacted his life and development. Before I hear that version, I have to know beyond a doubt that whatever his response might be, it will not alter or shake the firm foundation I have at last found. I am confident that regardless of his response or lack thereof, my security in who I am cannot be challenged. I am no longer fragile, vulnerable and able to be manipulated. His words will hold no power over me, except in a healing and forgiving way. There is nothing he can say to reduce me to the broken child I once was.

Jeremy had an acquaintance who, he believed, would know Father Michael's location. After a lengthy discussion with Jeremy, he agreed to inquire about Father Michael's whereabouts. A few days had passed since that conversation when an e-mail came across my computer. It listed a monastery in Northern Ireland as his presumed residence. My stomach started to swirl as if it knew the letters and numbers typed in that address were the closest contact with Father Michael I'd had in over twelve years. With the shakiness of an adrenaline rush, I immediately "googled" the monastery. I scanned their website, looking at all the pictures in hopes that I would catch a glimpse of him to confirm his location. I did not find his name or picture anywhere on the site, but did acquire an e-mail address and telephone number. I sent an e-mail stating I was looking for him and as I hit the 'send' button, prayed a silent prayer that this was the right move for me at the right time.

Every day after that, I hurried to check my e-mail for no other purpose than to look for that single response. A week went by with no response, so I sent a second inquiry. This time I realized that an answer might never come so I did not check my e-mail with the same eager anticipation. Then, one day, about a week and a half later, I checked my e-mail and there on my screen was the response I had almost given up. Unfortunately, the writer informed me that Father Michael had not lived at the monastery in years. He stated he wasn't really sure where he was, but had last heard he was living in a small, rural town. I thanked him for his efforts and then sat there pondering my next move. I questioned whether this was one of those God whispers encouraging me to stop the hunt because of pain and anguish that would come from digging up old skeletons. But then I listened closer to my heart. My spirit was screaming to me to keep searching. Any whispers coming from above were drowned by the relentless encouragement from within. I knew that regardless of the outcome, my heart could not find peace until I'd made an honest attempt to find and communicate with him.

The writer of the return e-mail did offer me a vague physical address to follow, and his correspondence indicated that I had a decent chance of finding him there. With the new information at hand, I began to draft a letter directly to Father Michael. Up to this point, there had been no attempt to think what I would say in that first letter. After three drafts, I settled on a letter that revealed my hope for communication, but did not disclose any personal information.

Despite completing the letter the same day I received the e-mail from the Monastery, it sat in my computer for a week before I summoned the courage to print it. Once the letter was printed, it took another week to address the envelope, and yet another to purchase the international stamp. I knew I was procrastinating, but couldn't confront it head on. I was having second thoughts. Once the letter was dropped in the mailbox, there was a real possibility that it would indeed arrive in Father Michael's hands. The man who caused so much heartache and pain in my life would now be able to respond in any number of ways. Was I *really* prepared to hear what he had to say? Would his response or lack of response push me backwards in my journey? Would it start a downward spiral that all the tools I learned in therapy could not stop?

I couldn't answer my questions and as each night came and my head hit the pillow, I conjured up every conceivable scenario. I was sleepless, watching the clock into the wee hours of the morning. When dawn came, my immediate thoughts continued my last thought before I had fallen into an exhausted slumber. I found myself irritated when my two-year old daughter ran into my room at first light to get me up with her incessant and adamant statement of "I'm 'hungee', Mama, get up." My anxiety was starting to affect my girls in the most direct way.

Wanting to keep my physical address private, I contacted Dr. Macey and asked if I could use her return address for all correspondence. She graciously agreed to be the conduit and offered to forward any mail received to my home address. For the same reason, I held onto the letter for a few more days after purchasing the stamp. I brought the letter with me to Dallas, where I traveled each week to work. I did not want the postal mark to be from my local address. I made a commitment to send the letter from Dallas, regardless of my reluctance. I did not want to live with an emotional block. Once the letter was sent, it literally was out of my hands and there was nothing to do but live my life and wait.

Months have passed with no response. I did not receive the original letter back, nor did I receive a response from Father Michael. I am left to assume that either he did not receive the letter or he simply chose not to respond. I will never know which, but am forced to accept it. Even without a response, there is peace in knowing I had the courage to try. I tackled my biggest fear and it has left me with a profound sense of accomplishment.

Chapter 21: Finding Closure

I consider myself blessed to have had the opportunity to meet with Father John nine years after my initial report of sexual abuse to the church. On a scheduled, routine visit back to home, I made an appointment with him. I wanted to share this book with him while it was still in progress. I wanted the opportunity to visit with him at a time when I was in balance, with my head screwed on straight. I had the benefit of therapy and hindsight to give me insight, wisdom and clarity. I was able to express gratitude for the money spent on therapy by the Catholic Church, specifically, Fr. Michael's religious order. Father John could see that the money spent was worthwhile and effective and I was able to tell him of my desire to give back to the world all I had received.

Our meeting allowed me to fill in gaps for myself and answer questions he had pondered over the years. The first time we met to discuss the accusations of sexual abuse, there was much I couldn't verbalize, but this time we had a free and clear dialogue about those events. The meeting cleared the air for both of us and left me with a sense that Grace really does overcome all.

As our visit concluded, Father John escorted me out of the building onto the breezeway. It was late February, but the day was sunny and pleasant. A gentle breeze brushed against my hair and the air smelled of spring. I made the comment to Father John that the physical grounds of the church had changed dramatically, so much so, that I'd had trouble finding his office. A new church had been built since my last visit. As we started down the breezeway, Father John pulled a set of keys out of his pocket, and while doing so, asked if I would like to see the new church.

I drew a deep breath, and said "yes, but you need to understand that this will be the first Catholic church I've in over a decade."

His response was genuine and a bit embarrassed. He said, "There I go again, assuming something may be comfortable when it is not."

I paused for a moment to reflect on his statement and then confidently assured him it was all right.

As soon as the door opened, I immediately became somber, reserved, and contemplative. Entering the empty sanctuary brought back those feelings and memories from long ago. I remembered the countless times I sat in an empty church asking, "Why am I so broken?" I also remembered and felt the devastation and disappointment at the lack of response to my prayers. Ironically, I did not think of Father Michael or the abuse endured. I was broken before he came into my life and it was the moments *before* I met Father Michael that came to mind. I often sat in an empty church deep in prayer, seeking solace. But on this visit, I was able to see, through the gift of hindsight, how God, so lovingly, answered each of one those prayers in the most perfect way. Gratitude filled my heart mixed with sadness for what was lost.

As I listened to Father John explain the symbolism in the stained glass windows that trimmed the tops of the walls, tears fell silently to the floor. I was speechless and deeply moved. Standing in that empty space allowed me to feel the loss of a religion and an identity that I once held so close. Even though I find peace and understanding in the Lutheran faith, I acknowledge that for most of my life, Catholicism was my faith… my identity. I felt a sense of loss and also nostalgia for something familiar from my past. Tears continued to drop to the floor as we walked up the incline to the back of the church to a small chapel. Father John looked at me with concern and asked whether it was right to have shown me the church. I reassured him that my tears didn't mean that it wasn't a good experience.

I had not been sure what my reaction to walking into a Catholic church would be because I'd never given myself the chance to find out. Walking into the church allowed me to discover what feelings bubbled up. I allowed myself to feel whatever crossed my heart. Our visit ended, leaving me with quiet acceptance of what was and what is. Despite my silent tears, our visit far exceeded my expectations in every way. I continue to pray that the visit with Father John provided him as well as me with understanding and gratitude.

God has blessed me with strength. Many times that strength was buried deep within my soul, unrecognizable, but I have found it and draw upon it daily. Through that strength, I have found Grace. After searching outwardly for all these years, I now turn inward and find peace in the fact that there is a loving God who knows every part of us, who knows our words before we speak them and understands them all. I feel safe in knowing that God loved us so much that he was willing to send his only Son to suffer and die in order to wipe away our sins. This is the essence of Grace. What parent is willing to watch their child die a painful death, no matter what good it could bring? Only the strength of God could offer such a thing. Being a mother has helped me to understand the true sacrifice He made.

The mistakes of my past, the hurts caused by others and by myself will always be a part of who I am. Those mistakes and hurts helped to form the person I am today, but it is the people who supported me through those times that ultimately contributed to my growth and development into a well-rounded, functioning adult who now plans to give back to the world all she has received.

At each step of this journey, I have introduced you to people who graciously entered my life and I have explained how each one had a unique purpose and role in my odyssey. There is a song often heard at Christmastime, sung by the country group Alabama. The title of the song is "Angels among Us." This songs speaks to my spirit because, during the work I have done with patients at the end of life, I have been graced with the presence of angels. I believe that all the spiritual mothers and fathers of whom I have spoken in this book are angels in disguise, sent here to help me in my darkest hours. The chorus of that song speaks, "Oh, I believe there are angels among us, sent down to us from somewhere up above. They come to you and me in our darkest hours, to show us how to live, to teach us how to give, to guide us with the light of love." I give thanks for all the spiritual mothers (and fathers) in my life: for Mrs. Winn, for Dr. Macey, for Lisa, for Megan, for Charles, for Kimberley, for Father John, for Jeremy, for Jacob and especially for my own mother who despite making some errors, has rebounded with all the love and support a mother can express. My mother has become my hero. As I look back on all she sacrificed for me during a time when she did not understand me or what was wrong, I marvel at her strength. She provided what I needed, no matter how difficult it might have been for her financially, emotionally, or spiritually. She is the best gift in my life and it is to her that I dedicate this book. I love you, Mom.

Epilogue

Nearly a year after the completion of this book, I continued my search for Father Michael through the internet. Each week, I flew back and forth to the hospice's corporate office to work. The many hours spent in airport terminals allowed me ample time for my research. Using the location given to me by the monastery, I looked up his name through Ireland's telephone directory found on the internet. His name and number appeared on the screen. How simple! But, was it accurate? I immediately dialed the number with my cell phone, but could not get the connection to work. Once I arrived at my office, I researched the country codes required to make an international call. Armed with this information, I stepped away from my desk to acquire better reception. As the phone was ringing, I walked to a near-by conference room under construction and stood near the glass windows. I was on the 16th floor of an office building in downtown Dallas, Texas. As I stood looking out the window at the traffic below, the ring tone was interrupted by a man saying "hello". Despite the many years since speaking with Father Michael, I knew instantly it was his voice.

"May I speak with Michael," I said hesitantly.

"Who is this? What is this about?" he said in a stern and defensive way.

"This is Crystal." I was relieved after all this time to have found him. When the relief subsided, absolute fear set in. The anxiety showed as I began to shake and sweat. Chest and face red once again.

"What do you want, Crystal?" I could hear the trauma and distrust in his voice.

"I want to know how you are and I want you to know how I am. I am in a space that allows me to hear whatever you might need to say to me."

"What's the point, Crystal? Do you want to know that I am not a priest anymore and that I still want to be?"

"Yes. I do want to know that, and I want you to know the challenges I faced, as well."

The conversation was intense; his words sharp.

"Put one foot in front of the other, keep going," I said to myself. "Stay present."

The conversation did *not* flow naturally, each word painfully expressed. His tone did not soften until I commented,

"You seem angry."

"No, no. No, I'm not angry," he said with a noticeable change in his tone. He could not maintain the softer tone as he said, "I'm not that kind of person. I would never do that to you! They said I 'groomed you. I'm not that kind of person!"

Collapsing to the floor at the sound of his words, I remembered his comments to me as an adolescent when I tried to confront him in the diner with the letter I had written. Tears welled in my eyes and a lump enlarged in my throat.

"I'm sorry; I'm sorry," I repeated as I cried, but instantly I became aware of the old patterns I was repeating.

Snapping out of it, I stopped apologizing and started confronting.

"How can you say that?" As I started to bring up specific instances, his voice softened, and he said,

"Well, I already apologized for that a long time ago." His voice trailed off into a mumble.

I became aware that he had not done the emotional and spiritual work to engage in such a conversation and realized we were in two separate spaces.

He changed the subject by asking if my parents were still alive. We talked about the health of my family, and for a brief moment, the anxiety and awkwardness was gone for both of us. It was a safe topic to discuss. I remembered how gentle our conversations used to be.

To my surprise, it was me who ended the call. Each time I would draw the conversation to a close, it was him who added a question or comment, as if he wasn't ready to end the call.

I concluded the call by offering his complete forgiveness. I shared with him that my daily prayers included him and my plans to continue to do so. I offered him my cell phone number should he ever have the courage to talk about our journeys, both together and separately. I made it clear to him that I could hear whatever he had the need to share and that I also wanted to share where my journey has taken me.

A year has passed since that phone call, and he has yet taken me up on my offer. I still welcome the call, but don't *need* it.

Just knowing whether he is alive or dead; working or not; healthy or sick has eased up so much space in my brain. I no longer lay awake at night wondering…wondering if I had the strength to talk with him; wondering if he was angry; wondering if he was still a priest. I could go on and on about all the thoughts that no longer occupy my mind. The encounter that I had feared and wished for proved to be valuable beyond expression. It took time to process his words and my reaction to them, but I am grateful for the opportunity.

I sleep peacefully at night knowing I did my part. Memories of him no longer infiltrate my thoughts. I feel happy, blessed, and loved, ready for what God has for me next.

LaVergne, TN USA
09 March 2010
175318LV00003B/6/P